Perceptive Tunes

Analysis of Indian Film Songs
(Part 1)

Harsh Thakkar

Contents

CONTENTS

Preface

The idea of song analysis stemmed from a discussion that took place with my teacher in a class of popular literature. I asked a question why Indian masala films seem to be so "mindless" and are often considered as something that you should watch by keeping your brain aside. She asked me to think if there is no moral dilemma or substance in commercial masala films of India. She gave me a task to analyze "Dil Dance Maare" from Tashan and I did watch the song. I realized how flawed my perception was. I then started a series of song analysis on my blog and social media. The response has been highly encouraging, particularly for the piece I wrote on "Beedi Jalaliye" from Omkara. As time progressed, I realized the depth that popular fiction had and how overlooked that depth is. Art for mass consumption is often equated to brainless and shallow creations that need no brain and are done just for the idea of making money. This may be true in some cases, but I believe that each piece of art has something deeper that makes it interesting and palatable for the common audience.

I narrowed down the idea of popular art analysis to one of the most popular and heavily consumed channels of media- Bollywood. I have been an ardent consumer of Bollywood songs since my childhood. Everyone I have talked to about Bollywood has had a very common perception that most Bollywood movies and songs often tend to please the audiences by just evoking emotions and do not have any deeper meaning to it. While I was studying mass media, there would be almost no one who would know or appreciate Bollywood movies as I would do. Everyone would talk about how Hollywood and western cinema is the best and is so layered.

To challenge these preconceived notions and highlight the depth, creativity, nuances, and intricacies of Bollywood, I am undertaking this idea of analyzing songs from popular Bollywood movies. I further narrowed down my area of analysis to songs because there has often been a hue and cry that Bollywood inserts songs mindlessly and they have no purpose other than to attract an audience and increase salability. Bollywood songs are poetry and music. The song can often function as a story in itself and add so many layers to the film. When the song is combined with visuals, it produces some fantastical imagery that pleasures the eye, ear, brain, and the soul.

Thus, the book is an attempt to uncover the depth and the beauty of the art that lies in the songs of Bollywood movies. It also tries to elevate the status of Bollywood songs, which is often not given the due it deserves. Lastly, the book also serves a personal purpose of combining my creative and analytical skills and giving it a permanent form that can be critiqued by the public.

One thing that I struggled with in this book was to come up with an idea as to how I can include images of the scene and the exact clips of the songs and the movies. I could make illustrations and I have tried to do that in the cover page as well but since it was not possible for me to cover each and every element, it is highly recommended to watch the song and then read the analysis. That would help you to focus on the song and understand what exactly I am talking about. There may be some instances where you might need to look at that particular scene which would be possible with the lyrics that I have attached.

I hope you enjoy this joyride that I have spent years polishing and updating.

Acknowledgments

I would like to thank my teacher, Dr. Susan Vivian George who helped me to explore popular literature in a way that I never had before. My heartiest gratitude also goes to Dr. Sarvar Sherrychand, a teacher of mine who helped unfold so many nuances and the intricacies present in the society that are often overlooked and neglected by people, sometimes due to conditioning and sometimes due to deliberate stigma. She has been instrumental in developing a feminist lens in my mind and making me dive deeper for relatively simple things.

An acknowledgement can never be complete without thanking my parents and friends. Ma has always supported me and been my biggest cheerleader. The seed of art, be it in writing, performing, or dancing or any form is the gift of my father who has always pushed me ever since my childhood. I do remember his pride when I used my writing skills to earn my pocket money while in college.

Bhavini Bhojani, my best friend has been instrumental in helping me take decisions to design the cover, push me through this process and finally enable me to publish this book which was in its draft mode since forever.

Raj Dasani has been my go-to person for anything and everything that needs some critical mindset. His honest opinions help me to be better.

Shifa Miyaji is the sweetest friend who helped me with writing the foreword and doing the herculean task of editing and proofreading.

Introduction

This book is a series of song analysis from various movies of the Indian film industry. I have tried to pick songs from various genres and time periods to induce the spice of variety and give you a versatile experience. For you to fully appreciate and relate to the lyrics, it is advised that you do watch the movie before reading any of the pieces. This would not only help you understand the analysis better but also give you a good cinematic experience.

There is a key that should be followed throughout the book for you to connect better.

Spoiler- The song analysis contains spoilers, and you should watch the movie before reading the post to have the best experience.

Recommended- It is recommended to watch the movie before reading the analysis. The song shall be enjoyed better in relation to the story as compared to its independent existence.

Independent- The song analysis can be viewed independently and there shall be negligible difference in your experience whether you have watched the movie or not.

The movies selected are mostly acclaimed movies that have been loved by the audience and the critics alike. However, there would be a brief synopsis of the movie given before the song analysis to refresh your memory if you have seen the movie.

Each song analysis shall cover three aspects in general. The video of the song, the lyrics, and the music are the major elements considered to present a wholesome perspective of the song.

Now, the journey of exploring the hues of Bollywood shall begin. Indulge in a perspective-based analysis of the songs and brace yourself to be stunned by the depth of art in a song that seems to be of a mere 5-minute time length.

1. Agar Tum Saath Ho-Tamasha

Tamasha-

Tamasha is a movie that is considered to be one of the best works of Imtiaz Ali. It shows us the journey of a person who is stuck with the idea of doing a corporate job while his passion and heart lies in the art of storytelling. The film encompasses the age-old tale of not being able to follow one's heart but in a way that is unique, layered, and supremely nonlinear.

Agar Tum Saath Ho is a song from Tamasha that is sung by Alka Yagnik and Arijit Singh. It is written by Irshad Kamil and composed by A R Rahman. This song comes in the movie when Tara finds Ved in the cafe and tries to patch up with him. However, Ved is still stuck in the rat race of life and finds it difficult to follow his heart. His conditioning prevents him from listening to his calling and he thinks that everything is worthless.

This song beautifully presents the conflict in Ved's soul. The heart wants to throw away the pretense of being a corporate worker and the mask of sophistication. The brain tells him that anything other than this would be as worthless and wasted as it is right now. This is wonderfully represented by two voices. Alka Yagnik's voice for Deepika and the character of Tara is the call of the heart. Arijit Singh becomes the call of the brain and the past experiences that Ved represents.

In fact, one can even view this song as the heart's last call to hold on and give it another chance before it enters an abyss of hopelessness and pessimism.

Pal bhar thahar jaao
Dil ye sambhal jaaye
Kaise tumhe roka karun
Meri taraf aata har gham phisal jaaye
Aankhon mein tum ko bharun
Bin bole baatein tumse karun
Agar tum saath ho..
Agar tum saath ho

Translation- Please wait for a moment so that my heart handles itself. How can I keep stopping you? Let every moment of grief leave me and let me fill my eyes with your image. I can keep talking to you without saying anything. If you are with me…

This is the call of the heart that says to hold on and give life another chance. It knows that things can get better and there is a lot to look forward to. However, it also understands the plight of the brain and the soul. It has gone through a lot and if it fails again, it will never get up again. Hence, the heart settles for a moment of life. This is perfectly evident in the first line that says to stop for Pal bhar. The helplessness and the exhaustion are described by Kaise tumhe roka karun. There is a desire to live life fully. If not for a lifetime, then just for a moment. The heart also knows that the task of living a beautiful life cannot be done alone.

Behti rehti..
Nahar nadiya si teri duniya mein
Meri duniya hai teri chaahaton mein
Main dhal jaati hoon teri aadaton mein
'gar tum saath ho

Translation- The rivers and canals of love flow in your world. My world is in your love. I mould myself in your habits.

The beauty of their companionship is presented in this paragraph. Rivers of happiness flow when they work with each other. It also shows the beauty of Ved living a life that he always wanted with Tara. Tara becomes the embodiment of heart, life, and desires for Ved. Ved is a complex human being with which Tara is extremely patient. Tara tries to unravel one knot at a time and discover the beauty of Ved. The beauty which even Ved is neither aware of nor acknowledges. Ved becomes the complex brain that functions in complex ways and is influenced by so many factors such as conditioning and society. The heart is a simple organ that knows what it wants and tries to get it. The synchronization of the heart and brain is achieved in Corsica when Ved and Tara meet. Ved shuns all his learnings and makes a fresh start when he says to not reveal their names or any personal details. This is where Tara recognizes the true Ved and connects with him. Their bond is unique and beautiful.

Teri nazron mein hai tere sapne
Tere sapno mein hai naraazi
Mujhe lagta hai ke baatein dil ki
Hoti lafzon ki dhokebaazi
Tum saath ho ya na ho kya fark hai
Bedard thi zindagi bedard hai
Agar tum saath ho
Agar tum saath ho

Translation- Your eyes have your dreams. Your dreams only disappoint me. I think talks of love are deception by lips. It does not matter if you are with me or not. My life was numb, and it shall be so.

This is the stanza that represents the ideas of Ved. Ved came back to Delhi and lived a normal life. He expected it to become better after returning from Corsica, but it did not. It became a happy dream that never came to life for him. He feels as if that is a fantasy, and it is over. Also, he feels that he has disappointed Tara by being someone so different than he was at Corsica. Tere Sapno mein hai Naraazi becomes a testament for those feelings. Ved's previous experience of narrating stories and listening to his heart was met with harsh reactions. This makes him think that listening to the desires and heart is worthless. He is also sidelining and suppressing his emotions as he is afraid to face the trauma again. Thus, he feels safe to lead a life of numbness and not risk being shattered by desires again.

Palkein jhapakte hi din ye nikal jaaye
Bethi bethi bhaagi phirun
Meri taraf aata har gham phisal jaaye

Aankhon mein tum ko bharun
Bin bole baatein tumse karun
'gar tum saath ho
Agar tum saath ho

Translation- My days go in a jiffy. I am running around in joy while I am sitting with you. Every grief falls away if I remember you and talk with your image. Only if you are with me.

This is the description of how blissful life can be in their unison. Grief would be away, and days would go in divine bliss. This is the description by Tara to convince Ved. This is the description by the heart to convince the brain. Their unison is the key to both of their happiness. There is no joy in separation. See how beautifully these lines represent the nature of the heart. Tara is the embodiment of a heart that never gives up. It can get tired and change its pace, but the beating is relentless. Tara does the same throughout the movie. She never gives up hope until the very end. However, she is happily convinced at the end of the movie. She was sad too and was always hopeful when they separated.

Teri nazron mein hai tere sapne
Tere sapno mein hai naraazi
Mujhe lagta hai ke baatein dil ki

Hoti lafzon ki dhokebaazi
Tum saath ho ya na ho kya fark hai
Bedard thi zindagi bedard hai

This repetition is a self-convincing talk by the brain to prevent giving into the desires. It acts as a rationale to not give in and hold his stance. The tone and the emotion behind this are that of sadness and numbness. He badly wants to give in to this desire. He is yearning for the day when he can do so but he is too afraid. He is like the child who was once bitten by a dog and is scared by the sight of a dog. The child cannot go to the dog even if he loves it badly and wants to pet it and play with it. Hence, he plays the past in the brain to prevent him from doing so.

Agar tum saath ho
Dil ye sambhal jaaye
(Agar tum saath ho)
Har gham phisal jaaye
(Agar tum saath ho)
Din ye nikal jaaye
(Agar tum saath ho)
Har gham phisal jaaye

Translation- If you are with me, my heart shall handle itself. My days pass in bliss if you are with me. Every grief slips away if you are with me…

The brilliance of this paragraph tells us the conclusion that we are going to witness. The brain ponders what can happen if he gives in to desires and the heart gives the perfect answers. In fact, see how perfectly it hurts both. *Dil Yeh Sambhal Jaaye* is the condition of the heart. It is restless and impatient. It craves peace but cannot find it. Their unison is the way to achieve it. The brain keeps pondering about what would happen if they united and the heart gives answers. The song ends with Har Gham Phisal jaaye, a line by the heart and the final answer to their woes and miseries.

Thus, the song presents a conflict of ideas and the dilemma of life through superb lyrics, excellent singing and a beautiful blend of music. Violins, piano, and flute are seamlessly blended to make a symphony of grief, sadness, and unfulfilled desires. That is the brilliance of Tamasha and all its creators.

2. Chali Kahani – Tamasha

<u>Recommended</u>

A clown introduces a robot. A robot that is walking the same old path and talking the same language. But, the robot has a heart. A heart that beats and desires to break away from conventions of the wired path. There begins the tale of Tamasha. There begins the song Chali Kahani. A song that not only establishes the ideology and the narrative that the film would follow but also dive deeper into the cultural and archetypal nuances that are ingrained in the minds of the audiences.

The drama begins by showing a child deeply fascinated by the art of storytelling. See how the idea of being a child is equated to not being accustomed and ingrained to the power of archetypes and having a fresh slate that can write any story that he wants to. He goes to the storyteller and asks him to tell stories. The storyteller tells stories that are canonical and archetypal. The ones that are known by everyone in the world in some form or the other.

Tirkit taal se lo chali kahani
Panghat kaal se lo chali kahani
Ho sarpat daudti hai fakt jubaani
Chhut-put aashiqui mein dhali kahani
Angin saal se hai wohi purani
Tere mere ishq ki ye nayi kahani
Aati kahaan se hai
Ye jaati kahaan kya pata..

Translation-

The story flows in a poetic rhythm. The same story that has been going on for ages. A saga that is transferred through generations via word-of-mouth storytelling. A saga of love stories. The love stories are the same as they were years before. No one knows where they come from and where they go.

Notice how the song starts with a high note. It is the beginning of Tamasha and the voice should be strong enough to captivate as well as attract new audiences. This paragraph sets the base of the Tamasha. It is an age-old story that has been going on. This Tamasha is not going to be the same. It would be very different from what one has observed. These lines set up the expectations of the audience and it goes on to give a recap about what stories one has heard and come across since ages.

Ye chenab ka dariya hai
Ye ishq se bharya
Wo leharon pe balkhati
Mahiwal se milne jaati
Wo naam ki sohni bhi thi
Mahiwal ki honi bhi thi

Translation- This is the river of Chenab. It is full of love and affection. She walked like the waves of Chenab and was going to meet Mahiwal. She was a girl named Sohni who was very beautiful. She was the lover of Mahiwal.

This is the first instance of the story. The narration starts with the classic example of the story of Sohni Mahiwal. A story that is immortal and known by everyone in India. This is a thread from which Tamasha starts. The very first lines tell us that like age-old classics, this shall be a love story too. But a different type of love story.

Lekin bhay kans ka tha usko
(toh phir)
Vasudeva ne kanha ko
(lekar)
Jamuna se paar langaaya..

Dariya se toh phiron ki
Behna ne phir Moosa uthaya
Chali kahani, chali kahani
Chali kahani, chali kahani

Translation- But they were afraid of Kansa, the evil king. Then Vasudeva took Krishna and crossed the Yamuna River. In the same way, Firaun's sister also took Moses from the river.

These lines establish the first connection and the common thread of an archetypal story. There was an evil king who was hell–bent on killing a newborn baby who was prophesied to claim the throne. People across the globe did the same thing- ensured the safety of the baby by giving it to a relative. Also, notice how beautifully the song is sung. Whenever the song reaches a part of tension and stress, the voice becomes full of chaotic and aggressive energy. When it reaches a part that is soft and symbolizes love, it is soft and soothing. Hear the lines – Dariya se to Phrion ki behna ne moosa uthaya and feel the change in the voice.

Just as this stanza gets over, the sargam of notes start. The love story of Sanyogita is shown. Notice how the storyteller says that she had crossed the boundaries of the society to meet her lover. The lines

" Chali Kahani, Chali Kahani" play on. They go on as the story goes forward but the kid stops the storyteller to correct the name of Sanyukta. This is the place where the storyteller tells the varied perspectives of speaking the same name. The dialect and the accent changes with region and even the name does but the idea remains the same. He gives various examples such as Jesus or Isa, or Sanyukta, Samyukta, or Sanyogita. He thus sows the seeds of what an archetype is in the mind of a young Ved.

It is just after this explanation on names that we notice a highly important and soothing flute tune. It is the tune of separation, pain, and longing. Also see how beautifully the tune sketches a graph of feelings in the song. The start was on a high note with full energy. There were instances when the notes were low and soothing but the tempo was fast and gave a sense of urgency. This is soothing yet evoking. The flute acts as a shift in the dramatic narration. Something is going to happen and this is the place where the emotions would be very different from what we have experienced.

Just as they complete this idea, the paragraph of Tirkit taal se Chali Kahani begins again. It symbolizes that no matter what one does and how badly one tries to stop, the story goes on. It also means the classic saying- the show must go on.

Birha ka dukh kaahe ho baanke
Dikhe mohe tu hi jo jiya mein jhaankiye
Pal pal ginti hoon aathon hi pahar
Kitne baras huey mohe haan kiye
Naina nihaaro more bhor se jhare (deepika)
Preet mori piya baaton se na aankiye
Main hi mar jaaun ya mare dooriyan
Dooriyon ki chadaron pe yaadein taankiye

Translation- Why are you upset about being separated? You are in my heart and I just need to peep in to see you. I count every moment of the day from the day I left you. Look at my eyes and you would see tears of love and longing. I cannot express my love through words so do not measure it there. Let me die or kill the distance. Sew the distance with the thread of memories.

This is the place where there is a drastic shift in the song. The singers have changed, and it is the voice of the actors in the narration. It is a conversation between two separated lovers. It is soft, melancholic, and a conversation full of longing that the two share. One talks about the impatience to meet others while the other convinces her to hold on and wait.

This stanza also completes the graph of the song. See how it started on a high and then fluctuated a bit in the song. The sargam becomes the midpoint where we hear changes and a sign of the coming difference. Just then, the Chali Kahani stanza is repeated, and the graph increases. This becomes the final low that is there in the song. What follows is another gush of energy and the climax of the song.

Wo utha virodhi parcham
Mughal-e-azam ko tha ye gham
Shehzada mohabbat karke
Izzat ka karega kachra bhasm
Roja ki thi helen
Tha ik mee raksha mein raavan
Antat bhishan yudhum krandan
Mera to ranjhan mahi ranjhan ranjhan

Translation- The rebellion flag was raised. The royal king was afraid that the prince would bring shame to the royal honor by loving someone outside their class. Helen was of Troy. Ravan was invincible and Sita was kidnapped by him. A deadly war was inevitable. All this happened for love and honor.

Thus, a damsel in distress is rescued by a prince charming, be it in Ramayana or the Trojan war. The epitome of a love story is portrayed when two lovers die for each other, just like Laila Majnu, Romeo Juliet, Heer Ranjha, or Sohni Mahiwal. The predicted saver of the kingdom is adopted by their relative, be it in the case of Krishna or Moses.

Listen to the song and you would also realize how dramatic and narrative it is. Music has its own journey. It has a soft flute beginning that lays the foundation for the story to start. Then there are notes on the brass and the vocals start blending with the brass notes. It then becomes a Jugalbandi of Sitar, percussion, and vocals that increase the tempo of the song and the excitement. As the second stanza starts, there is a perfect description of the start of a story, be it in the form of Krishna's birth or Moses' birth.

What follows is the Sargam that prepares us for what is coming next. There is a curiosity built to know more and impatience. Exactly then, there is a dip in the form of voice and the tempo when the stanza about Viraha plays. This is such a brilliant way to keep the audience hooked and give relief to the fast-growing tempo.

Finally, it reaches the climax of the song where the percussion and the vocals combine to beautifully give you the idea of excitement and thrill. The song ends with a high note, just as how a story ends with the victory of the archetypal hero.

Interestingly, the very next scene of the movie deviates from the archetypes. It is the scene where Ved and Tara meet and decide to not reveal their details, thereby starting the journey of deviating from conventions. What follows throughout the movie is how Tara plays an integral part in enlightening Ved's desire to be the storyteller and deviate from the conventions. And in turn, she becomes the person who does not need any prince charming to rescue her or she is not the embodiment of prince charming. She becomes the catalyst of his mind in a subtle yet powerful way, just like how the clown beats the robot on its heart and removes him from the boundaries of the treadmill.

That was a marvel from Tamasha. The movie is directed by Imtiaz Ali. This song is written by Irshad Kamil, composed by A R Rahman, and sung by Sukhwinder Singh, Haricharan, and Haripriya.

3. Bulleya – Sultan

<u>Recommended</u>

Sultan-

Sultan is a movie that shows the life of a wrestler who reaches the peak of his career but loses everything when blinded by arrogance. He loses the ability to fight, his love, and his own child.

Bulleya comes at a point in time in Sultan where all is lost, and Sultan's only hope left in life is to win the Mixed Martial arts championship that is being held in Delhi. Bulleya becomes the pivot that is the last contact with Aarfa, his wife and the last chance to ask for her forgiveness.

Kuch rishton ka namak hi doori hota hai
Na milna bhi bahut zaroori hota hai

Translation- The very essence of any relationship is the salt of distance.

Aarfa and Sultan have parted ways ever since Sultan was not present when his family needed him the most. This distance becomes the salt that becomes the catalyst for change. It is the separation that charges him to amend his life and take efforts to reconcile with Aarfa, and more importantly, himself.

Also notice how this is the point where there is no music yet and the lines act as a prologue to the song. The focus lies on noticing the depth of the voice and how upset, sad, and repenting it is.

Dum dum, dum dum tu mera
Dum dum, dum dum mera har

Translation- Aarfa is the breath of his life, and every heartbeat is hers. When she is not around, he feels dead.

This is perfectly reiterated later in Fateh Khan's remark, "I do not train dead people." The fight becomes a tool to win over Aarfa again and in a way, restart Sultan's life. Initially, Sultan chooses to wrestle to impress Aarfa and after that, he does it again to seek forgiveness.

Tu baat kare ya na mujhse
Chahe aankhon ka peghaam na le
Par yeh mat kehna arre o pagle
Mujhe dekh na tu, mera naam na le
Tujhse mera deen dharam hai mujhse teri khudai
Tujhse mera deen dharam hai mujhse teri khudai
Tu bole toh ban jaaun main Bulleh Shah saudai

Main bhi naachun (x2), manau sohne yaar ko
Chalun main teri raah bulleya
Main bhi naachun rijhaun sohne yaar ko
Karun na parwah bulleya

Translation- Whether you talk to me or not, whether you look at my eyes and ignore all my messages, please do not say that you never acknowledge or remember us when you spot me. You are my religion and you are my faith, if you say, I shall become Bulleh Shah. I shall dance, convince, and woo you and not care about anything else in the world.

Sultan is sure that Aarfa cares for him even when Aarfa is ignoring and not looking at him. He says that she is her God and Divinity. He can go to any extent and even trade his life if she wants him to. Notice how perfectly Sultan's face is full of hope and optimism when he sees her coming out from the mosque. This is literally how she is the source of his life. Looking at her makes his heart beat and even when he has lost all hope, she becomes the hope that makes him want to change things.

However, when she goes by not even acknowledging his presence, he is shattered again. Still, he does this daily and offers every bit, be it by dancing or by placating. The rejections would not matter to him and he would be carefree of the result of his pursuit. He would stop not until she is finally convinced of his guilt.

Mera har dum tu
Mera mehram tu, marham tu

...

Mera har dum dum har dum tu (x2)

He restates his love for her through these lines and says that she is his life, companion, and comfort. He gets a glimpse of her and feels alive. He does this every day to ensure that he is alive from inside and his emotions have not died.

Maana apna ishq adhura
Dil na ispe sharminda hai
Poora hoke khatam hua sab
Joh hai aadha woh hi zinda hai
Ho bethi rehti hai umeedein
Tere ghar ki dehleezon pe
Jiski na parwaaz khatam ho
Dil yeh mera wahi parinda hai
Bakshe tu joh pyar se mujhko toh ho meri rihaai (x2)
Tu bole toh ban jaaun main Bulleh Shah saudai

Translation- Their love is incomplete but there is no shame in its incompleteness. Every incomplete thing is alive while completion means death. His hopes are stuck at the gates of her house and his heart would wander like an aimless bird until she forgives him.

These lines act as a convincing point for Aarfa but in a way, Sultan is also convincing himself to live on. He is dead from inside and this acts as a push to live on and complete the incomplete story. His hopes might be stuck on Aarfa's gate but he is actually waiting for the moment when he is able to confront himself and finally be at peace with himself. When Aarfa will forgive him, there would be a ray of hope that if his lover forgave him, he can forgive himself too. Hence, his efforts are to face himself and finally come at an internal resolution.

Main bhi naachun...parwah bulleya
Mera har dum ... tu

Tu yaad kare ya na mujhko
Mere jeene mein andaaz tera
Sar aankhon par hai teri naraazi
Meri haar mein hai koi raaz tera
Shayad meri jaan ka sadka maange teri judaai (x2)
Tu bole toh ban jaaun main Bulleh Shah saudai
Main bhi …. Bulleya
Kuch rishto...hota hai

Translation-It does not matter if you remember or forget me, your way of living is imbibed in me. I understand and acknowledge your disappointment in me. Maybe there is some reason for my loss and that led to the separation.

He realizes that it is possible to forgive himself because a part of Aarfa that resides in him. He has become a better person with her love. He understands her feelings of contempt towards him. He believes his ignorance has cost him his life. Maybe their separation demands a sacrifice of his life which he is ready to give if she says.

It is interesting to see how he juxtaposes his own disappointment and Aarfa's disappointment in him through this song. He is having glimpses of life in his ditch of internal death. Aarfa becomes that ray of light that he holds on to and tries to climb out of the dark ditch. However, he also realizes that he would not be able to climb out of it until he convinces himself that he deserves to get out of it. He does not get convinced until the last fight of the movie wherein he is able to defeat the final opponent-himself.

4. Bum Bum Bole - Taare Zameen Par

Independent

Taare Zameen Par-

Taare Zameen Par can be considered as one of the most revolutionary films in Indian cinema. Released in 2007, it acted as a catalyst to bring about some great changes in the Indian Education system. From spreading awareness about learning difficulties such as dyslexia to shedding some light on the mental stress that a student faces in the modern educational context, the film has had a wide reaching impact. It is almost impossible to grasp the whole idea of the film without watching it but a song from the movie- "Bum Bum Bole" does a commendable job of how a bit of change in the system and pedagogy can bring about life changes in students.

The song starts with some flute notes being played and the children are alerted. They stop playing and doing masti and are curious to find out where the noise is coming from. As they figure out that it is a voice coming from the direction of the door, they are curiously looking at the door and Ram Shankar Nikumbh (Aamir Khan) enters with a boo. He does some acrobatics and goes near the children and tries to scare them again with voices and grunts. As they are caught by surprise, the children rush to their seats and are frightened. Here, it is also important to note the attire and the get up that Nikumbh has worn. The costume of a circus clown makes it a really interesting thing to note. Clowns are associated with humour in the circus and also horror in films like the IT or the batman series. The duality of this is perfectly highlighted as Nikumbh first scares them and then takes on the task of singing in gibberish some rhyming words. The gibberish has the students amused and they figure out that there is nothing to fear in this person. To assure the same, Nikumbh first removes the fake nose and then starts playing the flute.

The flute is an essential element here. In the beginning, it acts like a soothing agent but they have no idea as to where it comes from. The flute also acts as an entry point for Nikumbh. He wants to be just like the flute- soothing and peaceful. However, in order to realize his calmness and peace, there needs to be chaos. The chaos that is created by his dramatic entry of scaring and shocking the children. Note how the contrast is not only for this surface and song but also has a far-reaching impact in the movie itself. The teachers that the students have been taught from have followed the similar pattern of lecturing. A lecture which more or less sounds like gibberish to the kids unless they pull themselves to listen to it carefully and keep themselves focused on it. The laughter of the kids is the perfect mockery of it. There is no sense that it makes and it becomes just a mere rhythm of sounds which sounds pleasing. The difference is that when Nikumbh makes it, it is much more amusing as compared to any other teacher- something that is later proved and highlighted throughout the movie, especially with Ishaan Avasthi. The gibberish ends while Nikumbh has taken a full round of the class and has reached the centre. It is then concluded with a signal of shush which is then reciprocated by the students. Notice how quickly the students have started syncing with Nikumbh and reciprocating him except Ishaan. This is then accompanied by the removal of nose and playing of the flute notes- suggesting the lifting of the mask and creating his own identity. The flute notes are entertaining and soothing. They grab the attention and the attention is not enforced, something that the students find missing in every other teacher.

Nikumbh's character has left an impression and managed to become a favourite of the children in just a span of a minute by entertaining them and presenting them with a variety of emotions and expressions. Each of his actions is attention grabbing and entertaining. A song is often used in various Bollywood movies to introduce a character – usually, they are more theme based and lack lyrics which is not the case here.

Dekho dekho kya woh pedh hai

Chaddar odhe ya khada koi

Translation-
Look, is that a tree
Or is it someone covered in a blanket

The first stanza is just a question that allows the children to think in an unusual manner. Nikumbh goes to the window and points it out to the children. They are observing the tree very carefully and want to answer his question soon. This paragraph also becomes an entry point of the children to his ideology. They are presented with an opinion and an option to look at something very mundane like a tree in an unusual manner. This is yet another stroke that paints the picture of Nikumbh to the audience and the children. An unusual view towards everyday things is not only shared but also encouraged. The very language of the song- a question or an option is suggestive of the openness to multiple expressions as compared to simple facts or opinions. There is also the scope of debate that he invites by saying if his view matches with theirs or not.

Hey dekho dekho kya woh pedh hai
Chaddar odhe ya khada koi
Baarish hai ya aasmaan ne
Chhod diye hai nal khule kahin

Translation- Look, is that a tree
Or is it someone covered in a blanket
Is it the rain falling
Or has the sky opened some taps

The first stanza has introduced us to his ideology and now we are presented with more insights of the same. He gives us another question to think about. This time, it is about rain. Whether it is raining or someone up in the sky left the tap open. Instead of telling, he is asking. This is a really fundamental thing that would not only enable them to pay attention but also think about the same. By changing the role from a provider of answers and facts to becoming a person who questions and enables thinking, he is enabling self-discovery. It is proven that the things that a person discovers and learns by themselves are less likely to be forgotten as compared to what others tell them. In fact, the constructivism theory by Jean Piaget [1] states the same. The theory emphasizes experiential learning and learning through cognitive associations like role playing and toys. That is what we see Nikumbh doing here. He is asking questions and setting a goal to achieve. How they achieve, when they achieve, and why they achieve it is their lookout and choice.

Hum jaise dekhe yeh jahan hai waisa hi
Jaisi nazar apni
Khul ke soche aao
Pankh zara phailao
Rang naye bikhrao
Chalo chalo chalo chalo
Naye khwaab bhun le

Translation-

The world is what you make of it
It's in the eye of the beholder
Come let's think openly
Spread your wings
Spread new colours
Come on now
Let's weave new dreams

Adding to the comfort and amusement that he has already provided the children; he says that it is the perception that creates the world. It becomes what you look at it as and how you look at it. There is no perfect definition of the world and it is what you see in it. Open mindedness and multitude of perceptions is what he is looking at here. He says that these ingredients would make the recipe for a young brain that is always coming up with new thoughts and dreams that are unheard and unthought about.

If the lyrics present the mental openness of Ram Shankar Nikumbh, the visuals and the dance of his shows the physical openness of his. From the beginning of the song, he has been moving around the class and engaging every student in what he does. His entry was through some acrobatic flips- something that would be considered as a complete blunder for a teacher to perform in a traditional classroom. The flips then transform to dance and singing. Art does not stay to the confines of brush and paper but it takes the omnipresent form- dance, write, sing, move, and express. As he moves around the class, he engages with every student in some form or the other. He showers confetti on one, plucks the nose of one, puts a moustache on another. This is also a very open stance of his that he includes anyone and everyone. A very symbolic representation of welcome and acceptance is how his clown costume gets distributed to several students of the class. Each becomes a new person with an idiosyncrasy of their own. Do note how clowns perform acts and gigs that are odd and unusual in nature that make a person laugh. Nikumbh's ideology then becomes the costume that was once all his but now has been distributed in parts to everyone in the class. They pick up what they like and wear it with pride, while dancing with the teacher.

On the other hand, Damodar tries to encourage Ishaan to go and join the dance, but Ishaan is least interested in that. This is also very symbolic and striking. Although the teacher is trying his best to use unconventional methods to include everyone, he is not successful because Ishaan is reserved. Ishaan's reservation stems from the constant dismissal and disrespect that is shown to him by other teachers. He has now no hopes left from anyone, and he has even tried to commit suicide just before the entry of Nikumbh. The previous experiences have created a mental shield that prevents him from engaging in any new experience however promising they may be. The amount of disinterest and hopelessness shown through a child is a profound symbol of the effect of an archaic educational system on mental health- so much so that even when someone offers help, there is no hope to take it.

Even the Sargam that they sing- something that is a form of classical music and often taught with strict discipline, is taught with ease and fluency in a very relaxed and fun manner. Something that is the ideology of Nikumbh.

Bum bum bole ... bum bum bole
Hey bum chik bole ... bum chik bole
Arre masti mein dole ... masti mein dole
Bum bum bole, masti mein dole

Bum bum bole, masti mein tu dol re

Translation-
Swing along and shake a leg (x2)
Swing along and shake a leg
Have lots of fun
Swing along and have lots of fun
Sing along and you have lots of fun (x2)

Fun is what he wants to serve and have. In fact, this is stated precisely in the scene that follows the entry. He is in the staff room where other teachers pass remarks of his singing, dancing, and unorthodox style to which he replies that if they had fun and I had fun, that is what I want and more than enough.

Bhala machliya bhi kyun udhti nahi
Aaise bhi socho na
Socho sooraj roz nahaye ya
Baal bhigoke yeh budhoo banaye hume
Yeh saare taare timtimaye
Ya phir gusse mein kuch badbadate rahe

Translation-
Why can't the fishes fly
Think in that manner as well
Does the sun bathe every day
Or does it just wet his hair and fools us

Do all these stars shine
Or are they grumbling in anger

If the first few stanzas were questions with options, these lines become a direct challenge to conventions. He is not only challenging the conventions but also questioning the very need and existence of them. He starts with something that is very basic and evident such as the natural phenomena. Flying fishes, bathing sun, blabbering stars are all images of art that try to give an alternate perspective. Although they present a different view, they also lead towards a more scientific and experimental thinking attitude that relies on facts and proofs instead of simple authoritarian information. The emphasis on "socho" (think) as compared to "yaad karo" (rote learn) is present throughout the song. He wants them to think and question everything that is taken for granted as a fact.

Khul ke soche aao
… Bum bum bole, masti mein tu dol re

O rat rat ke kyun tanker full
Tanker full, tanker full
Aankhen band toh dabba gul

Oye dabba gul, dabba gul
Oye band darwaze khol re

Khol re, khol re, khol re

Ho ja bindaas bol re
Bol bol bol bol bol re
Main bhi hoon ... main bhi hoon

Tu bhi hai ... tu bhi hai
Main bhi, tu bhi, hum sab milke
Bum chik ... bum bum chik (x3)
Bum bum bole, masti mein dole (x2)

Translation-

Why cram until your head is full
Head is full, head is full
And you forget all if you close your eyes
Forget all, forget all
Open the doors that are closed
Open them, open them, open them
Say it without any fear
Come on say it
I'm also there ... I'm also there
You're also there ... you're also there
You, me, we all are there together to
Swing along and shake a leg
Swing along and have lots of fun

This stanza is a huge contrast to what has been established and was being talked about. It is not only lyrically different, but also has different music. The soothing yet pleasurable beats accompanied by a melody of joy is now replaced by a harder percussion-based music where you can also hear the shrill drum beats. Although this blends in perfectly with the previous music and beats, there is a difference between how the two have effect on the ears. The previous beats would not bother or affect in a stressful way but these have a slight tendency to do that with thicker and in your face style beats.

The lyrics show how they have been accustomed to rote learn and memorize like robots. So much so that they forget the things that they have learned just a second after they do so and close their eyes. It is time to open new doors and speak the language of the heart which is not only easy to understand but also easy to remember and mould it in one's own style. So, when two people who are keenly interested in knowing things and opening new doors, they should come along and dance to the tunes of learning.

Aaisi rangon bhari apni duniya hai kyun
Socho toh socho na
Pyar se chunke in rangon ko
Kisi ne sajaya yeh sansar hai
Joh itni sundar hai apni duniya
Upar waala kya koi kalakar hai

Translation-
Why is our world so colourful
Just think about it
Selecting these colours with love
Someone has decorated this universe
Since our world is so beautiful
Is God some form of an artist

The concluding stanza does multiple things- instils a sense of gratitude and awe in listeners, restates Nikhumbh's ideology of open thinking, and also introduces them to the world of art and colours. He not only wants to thank God but also wants the children to think how meticulously and perfectly God has designed the world. Just like how God is the ultimate artist, we can also try to do the same in whatever means we can and express ourselves as freely and openly as we can. That would be the ultimate victory of God. Do note how cleverly he mentions thinking and design of the God in the same way. It is not that he is saying that accept what is made and does not question it but thinks of the details and the intricacies that God considered while making this world. While thinking about it, you would get questions and you would go on a journey to find the answers by yourself- thereby fulfilling the ultimate task of a teacher and a guide like Nikumbh. And in order to facilitate that and encourage that, he says-

Khul ke soche aao
Pankh zara phailao
Rang naye bikhrao
Chalo chalo chalo chalo
Chalo chalo chalo chalo
Naye khwaab bhun le
Bum bum bole, masti mein dole
Bum bum bole, masti mein tu dol re (x3)

And calls them to join him in the ultimate fun activity – a journey of lifelong learning.

Thus, Taare Zameen Par proves to be a movie that not only entertains but also enlightens. Its enormous success in the box office can be attributed to the relativity that many parents found and the fact that the teaching method of Nikumbh perfectly resonates the ideas of education as laid out by the National Curriculum Policy of 2005. (Jena) [2] No wonder the song becomes an essential part of the masterpiece that is created.

References –

1. Wikipedia Contributors. "Constructivism (Philosophy of Education)." Wikipedia, Wikimedia Foundation, 15 Mar. 2019, en.wikipedia.org/wiki/Constructivism_(philosophy

_of_education)

2. JENA, PRAJNYA PARAMITA. "National Curriculum Framework 2005, Constructivism and Inclusion in the Face of Indian Film."

Film, Song). "Bum Bum Bole (Full Song) Film - Taare Zameen Par | Shaan, Aamir Khan." *YouTube*, 24 May 2011, youtu.be/NJ1NIIdHhXs Accessed 13 Nov. 2020.

5. Ek Lau- Aamir

Aamir-

Aamir is a story of an ordinary doctor who has returned to India from London. His family is kidnapped by a group of extremists who make him do several things that he does not want to. Aamir becomes a tale of courage, bravery, and the love for family. It symbolizes a lot of things, especially how religion is viewed as a trigger for and against some radical actions. It is indeed one of the finest movies in Indian cinema with a gripping and tightly packed narrative.

Ek lau comes as a credit song in the movie. Please note that this song analysis is full of spoilers and you do need to watch the movie in order to enjoy this analysis. I hope you do so and get the full idea of the write up.

The song starts with very repetitive and high-pitched notes on the guitar. It is soon joined by notes on flute. This is the perfect build up and the base to signify the sadness of the song. The flute notes are very striking and the main element that represents the sadness.

The sadness is of loss, but more importantly a loss of something that is unfinished and has the potential to make a difference in the world. This is then joined by an electronic instrument which plays the same notes in a different pitch. This heightens the impact and adds to the element of grief and heartbreaking emotions.

Gardishon Mein Rehthi,
Behti Guzarti.
Zindagiaa hein Kitni,
In Mein Se Ek Hai,
Teri Meri Ankahee,
Koi Ek Jaisi Apni..

Translation-There is one life amongst the many in motion whose story is unsaid and unheard, a story that is just like yours and mine.

The crux of this movie and song is the relatability that it brings to the viewers. The story of the person is very ordinary and can happen to any of us. This song does a brilliant job of taking a closer look at a story that is different and unsaid. It reveals sadness to us by saying the things in the past. The usage of past tense is the pain point. A story is left unfinished and the writer of that story left us to save humanity.

Par khuda khair kar aisa anjaam
Kisi rooh ko na de kabhi yahaan
Gujhaa muskurataa hai kyun waqt
Se pehele kyun chhod
Chalaa teraa ye jahaan

Ek lau is taraah kyun
Bujhi mere maulaa
Ek lau zindagi ki maulaa (x2)

Translation-Oh lord, do not give this type of end to any soul! A blooming flower decayed before its time. Why has a flame extinguished so badly? A flame of life, my lord!

The second stanza directly talks about the end and the result of his life. Aamir has lived such an ordinary life but his end has been so cruel and ruthless. He had so much life and desires that got extinguished before time. This a direct question to God but more importantly, it becomes the question to our own selves that why do we do these kinds of acts? Where has humanity vanished that we indulge in such gruesome acts? The timing of the song is perfect. It comes after Aamir decides to remove the suitcase containing the bomb and sacrifice his own life in a distant area with no one around. He had no intentions of malice and he was one who got badly mingled in the dilemma of survival.

Dhup ke ujaale si oans ki pyaale si
Khushiyaan mile hum ko
Zyada mangaa hai kahaan
Sarahaden naa ho jahaan
Duniya mile ham ko
Par khudaa khair kar
Us ke armaan men kyun
Bewajah ho koi qurbaan
Gujhaa muskuraataa hai kyun
Waqt se pehale kyun chhod
Chalaa tera ye jahaan

Ek lau is taraah kyun
Bujhi mere maulaa
Ek lau zindagi ki maulaa

Translation -May we get the sunshine of happiness and the sweet dew of life. We only wish for a world without boundaries. Oh lord, please save anyone sacrificing themselves for this cause without reason! Why should a blooming flower decay before time and leave the garden of life? Why has a flame extinguished so badly, My lord? The flame of life, my lord...

The last stanza does a wonderful job of conveying the perfect message of the movie. Why should someone be killed for the sake of eliminating discrimination and differences? All we desire is a world of harmony and peace. A world without borders of hate and apathy. Aamir becomes the leader who has sacrificed himself and chose to make a difference in the world by backing out at the last moment. He faced the dilemma of his life. He could either save himself and his family or he could save hundreds of innocent strangers and the differentiation between the religions. He becomes the perfect human here. He chooses his own life to sacrifice instead of letting hundreds die and sowing the seeds of hatred. He is the perfect Muslim who chose to help humanity instead of sparking communal hatred and burning the fire of death. This not only portrays the true role of religion in saving people's life, both literally and metaphorically but also becomes the ultimate message of humanity-

To not cut throats in the name of religion.

This idea is very basic and simple. No one should die for this and the song pinpoints this idea. The very need of someone to sacrifice themselves in order to create a better world is a mockery of life. No one needs to teach people. Everyone is sane enough to realize the flaws and live in a better world.

But alas, someone has to fight the wars, someone has to stop the riots, and someone has to imprison people so that others can live peacefully. This is the irony of life. This is the irony of humanity. And this is the irony of religion.

Ek lau is taraah kyun

Bujhi mere maulaa
Ek lau zindagi ki maulaa

As the stanzas end here, the song goes on with the message of ek lau bujhi to reinstate the idea of humanity and grief of its death. We also hear a new voice joining the female one. This becomes such a symbolic representation of how the idea of humanity and the quest for a better world is taken over by another person who is equally moved by the tragedy of human actions. The story not only moves the person but also becomes the call to action for him. The music is a fast-paced set of percussion notes at the end. This is the working of the brain. The person who has joined the cause is thinking of this state of the world and is so engrossed in the thought that the thought has overpowered him and has made him go in a state of deep thinking and the state of the idea to something for humanity. The percussion notes are then joined by the tragic flute ones that remind the person that it is very important to something urgently and immediately or this might be repeated. The flute notes also signify the impact that he has had and how the tragedy has stuck his heart and soul. Violin also joins the band of instruments to symbolize how tragic and grief-stricken is the state of affairs. The notes also become a constant reminder that the world is full of such tragedy and there is no escape from this. The violin notes also signal the end of the song and the end of a radical mindset. There is finally some hope that one can expect. This is resonated by the few keyboard notes that play on the exact end of the song.

Aamir has become the leader of something that will happen soon and he becomes the leader that inspired the people to walk on the path of humanity, no matter how tough it is.

6. Ek Pal Ka Jeena- Kaho Na Pyaar Hai

<u>Independent</u>

Kaho Na Pyaar Hai-
Kaho na traces the story of a girl whose boyfriend is murdered and then she finds a doppelganger of her

boyfriend who helps us to avenge the murder.

20 years ago, a song came and became a rage among the generation. The song did two most remarkable things- revolutionized the dance in Bollywood and introduced an actor who became the heartbeat of many in just a second. The song is" Ek Pal Ka Jeena" from the blockbuster Kaho Na Pyaar Hai.

This song became the pulse of the nation then and caught the attention of everyone. The unique and mysterious voice of Lucky Ali combined with the buttery dance of Hrithik engraved a place in everyone's heart: from the children to the grandmas and grandpas. This song analysis is a tribute to the film and the actor. The dance is breathtaking and the lyrics are deep. However, you would be fascinated to know how intricately the story of the film goes along with the song and how the song is a leitmotif (a theme) of Raj (the US version of Hrithik in the film).

The song starts with Amisha Patel entering the discotheque. The music is light and soothing with pan flutes and percussion playing in the background. Exactly before Hrithik is shown in the frame, there are drumbeats that reveal him and introduce him. This is a very nice move that builds up a curiosity to see the person. The same curiosity is felt by Sonia (Amisha Patel) when she notices the bike that Raj was driving before. Here, she is staring at the person to see if it really is Rohit. The drums break out and a tune on guitar plays. The guitar strokes are iconic. They are the leitmotif, that is, a small melody or arrangement of notes that are played when a character or a scene is shown. A simple example of the same can be the background music "Nikka" played whenever Komolika of Kasuati Zindagi Ki came on the screen with her destructive ideas and antagonistic thoughts. The guitar strokes are catchy as well as mysterious. They create a mystery in the minds of the viewer as well as the mind of Sonia. Notice how the tune prolongs and the pan flute also becomes a part of the same theme. The tease goes on for a few seconds when he is shown dancing but in the shadows. His body movements and body are shown but the face is not. The shadow covers the face for the time until the lyrics start.

The mystery is created by the curiosity evoking music and the shadow play on the introduction of Raj.

Ek pal ka jeena, phir toh hai jaana
Tohfa kya leke jaiye dil yeh batana
Ek pal ka jeena, phir toh hai jaana
Tohfa kya leke jaiye dil yeh batana
Khali haath aaye the hum
Khali haath jayenge
Bas pyar ke do meethe bol jhilmilayenge

Translation

We live for a moment and then we have to go
O heart tell me, what gift can I take with me
We live for a moment and then we have to go
O heart tell me, what gift can I take with me
We had come empty handed
We'll leave empty handed
We'll just sing a few words of love
So laugh, as we have to make the world to laugh

As soon as the lyrics start, the face is shown. See how aptly the first line fits the face. "Ek Pal ka jeena, phir to hai jaana, Tohfa kya leke jaiye dil yeh batana." This is a perfect memory of Rohit who lived a short life and was killed. What gift could he give but love? That is exactly what Rohit does. He is in love with Sonia and Sonia with him. They are happy until he is killed. Also, Rohit is a simpleton who would do anything to make Sonia happy. He wants to help people and make everyone happy. Hence, *"Bas pyar ke do meethe bol jhilmilayenge, Toh has kyun ki duniya ko hai hasana ".* Stay happy as I want to help the world and make everyone happy.

Ae mere dil tu gaaye jaa
Ae aaye aao aaye aa

Ae mere dil tu gaaye jaa
Ae aaye aao aaye aa

Translation-

Hey my heart, you keep on singing
(Music beats)
Hey my heart, you keep on singing
(Music beats)

These lines are his life philosophy of letting the heart sing and do what feels right. Additionally, Raj is happy but ignorant about the fact that he looks like Rohit and Sonia is worried about it. His ignorance is making him happy and he is singing a song of bliss. He is happy in his world. Notice how the lyrics end and the music becomes more mysterious and teaseful. It builds suspense and creates tension. A contradiction in the minds of the audience as well as Sonia about the presence and the existence of this guy who died before. The music is recurring throughout the song and there is no resolution of it in the song. It only gets resolved later in the movie.

O aankhon mein dilbar ka sapna bhi hai

Haan koi sapna bhi hai

O duniya mein mera koi apna bhi hai

Haan koi apna bhi hai

Ek chehra khaas hai

Joh dil ke paas hai

Hothon pe pyaas hai

Milne ki aas hai
Dilbaron ka magar kahan koi thikana

Translation -

There is a dream of my beloved in my eyes
Yes, there is a dream
There is also a dear one of mine in this world
Yes, there is also someone who is dear to me
There is a special face
Which is close to my heart
There is thirst on my lips
There is a hope to meet her
But you can't trust these beloved ones

If the previous lines were of ignorance and detachment from Sonia and her world, these lines are a striking contradiction to them. There is a hope of meeting his dream girl and his lover. Raj is thinking about a girl who is madly in love with him and he with her. Also, these lines show a possibility of him falling in love with Sonia at the first sight when they met before on the road at the traffic signal. Notice how there is a transition from the dance of Raj to Sonia on words such as Sapna and apna. The dramatic irony here is the fact that Raj is totally in love with her but for Sonia, he is already someone whom she knows, hence, the focus on Apna is brilliant. Raj wants to express his love to her while she is confused about what is happening and why does he look and feel familiar. He is excited and restless to meet her and talk to her. A hope of union keeps his love alive. However, he refutes his own idea by saying that love is not to be trusted and lovers are wanderers. This is also a rational response of the brain to the fact that he likes Sonia and wants to get close to her but his mind prevents him from doing so and tells him to be practical and realistic. The stanza ends with the chorus hook-line of the heart's singing and the mysterious music follows for a while.

O jeevan khushiyon ka ek jhaunka sa hai
Haan koi jhaunka sa hai
O aur yeh jhaunka ek dhoka sa hai
Haan koi dhoka sa hai
Yeh kaisi hai Khushi
Jal jalke joh bujhi
Bujh bujhke joh jali
Milke bhi na mili
Doston par kisi haal mein na ghabrana

Translation-
Life is like a gust of happiness
Yes, like a gust
And this gust is deceptive
Yes, it's deceptive
What kind of happiness is this
What got extinguished after burning fast

What started burning after extinguishing
What I didn't attain even after achieving it
But friends, in any case don't be scared

Life is like a breeze of happiness to both here. Sonia is happy yet puzzled that she has found Rohit again. It is a breeze of joy for her. Raj is happy that he finally has seen and met his dream girl. The happiness of finding her is what makes him excited. However, the breeze is deceptive. Both the people are thinking of each other as their lovers but in reality, things are different. Sonia is seeing Rohit in Raj. She is replacing Raj with Rohit. Raj does not exist for Sonia and it is only Rohit that she sees in him. Deception for Sonia is the existence of another person who is the doppelganger of Rohit. She doesn't believe that and considers him as Rohit. When it comes to Raj, his intentions are straightforward and not puzzled as Sonia. He is head over heels for Sonia and considers her response as a positive sign to his approach. Although he recognizes that she has a puzzled look every time she sees him, he cannot think of the extreme thought that she has. He is happy in his approach and satisfied that she is responding. His deception is the response that she is giving to him which is actually just figuring out the truth. His happiness is changing forms. He has finally met his dream girl but the union is based on an assumption. The love is not pure as she considers him Rohit. *"Jal jalke joh bujhi"*- the hopes rising and falling. *"Bujh bujhke joh jali"*- they finally accept each other later in the film as they are and are united. He has finally found her and become her lover but his happiness is halfhearted as she is still not fully his and dedicated to Rohit. The positivity and the happy go lucky attitude of Raj is shown again in the lines- *Doston par kisi haal mein na ghabrana*. He is optimistic about everything.

The rain shower starts in the stanza of a spark burning and extinguishing, again a symbolization.

A really interesting thing to notice about this stanza is the pouring rain. The visual is perfectly placed with the lines of burning and extinguishing. Also, Sonia is never shown in this stanza in the discotheque symbolizing the difference and the distance they have in their perceptions about each other. He keeps dancing as the chorus lines repeat and the lyrics end. The music is still on with the mysterious guitar notes accompanied with the clever pan flute. Raj approaches Sonia and they both have a puzzled, curious, questioning expression with eyes that are searching for answers. The song ends on that tone with an aalap from Lucky Ali that adds to the mystery. It enhances the curiosity and adds to the puzzle that they both are trying to solve.

The Mystery reaches its peak when the two have an eye contact and Raj is going to approach her. This is accompanied by the tune of the song along with Lucky's Aalap that enhances the mystery.

Thus, the song that introduced the world to a future heartthrob isn't just a mere dance number but a song of brilliance created by Rajesh Roshan, Lucky Ali, Ibrahim Ashq, and the lead actors- Hrithik Roshan and Amisha Patel.

7. Beedi – Depth Masqueraded Under an "Item Number" (Omkara)

<u>Spoilers</u>

Omkara-

Omkara is the story based on Othello. Omkara is a gangster and Langda Tyagi is one of the generals in the gang. Omkara becomes the next general of the gang. Langda Tyagi feels upset and frustrated as his post is being usurped by Omkara. He instigates Omkara that Omkara's wife is cheating and the movie unfolds what happens as a result of this.

I remember the time when this song was released and I

hated it because of its rustiness and the rowdy visualization. After like 10 years, I learnt how to appreciate and be mesmerized by this song. However, it was not until a few days back that I stopped looking at it as a well written and well-placed item number and realized how deep and perfectly made the song is considering the context and the placement of it. I have now decided to debunk this misconception of it being a stupid item number that is done for viewership's sake in order to highlight its beauty and the depth that it masquerades so beautifully.

Let us look at the lyrics and see how intricately it is woven with the visualization and the story of Omkara.

Na ghilaf, na lihaf
Na ghilaf, na lihaf
Thandi hawa bhi khilaf sasuri
Na ghilaf, na lihaf
Thandi hawa bhi khilaf sasuri
Itni sardi hai kisi ka lihaf laile
Ja padosi ke chulhe se aag lai le
Ja padosi ke chulhe se aag lai le

Translation-

I don't have a sheet nor a quilt
I don't have a sheet nor a quilt
Even the damn cold air is against me

I don't have a sheet nor a quilt
Even the damn cold air is against me
It's so cold that take a quilt of someone
Go and take some heat from the neighbor's fire
Go and take some heat from the neighbor's fire

The song starts with Kesu/ Cassio (Vivek Oberoi) singing the lines and starting the song. He is soon followed by Langda Tyagi/ Iago (Saif Ali Khan) who repeats the same lines that Kesu sang. Note how the hierarchy of their posts with regards to their gang position is also reinforced through the singing. The 'Bahubali' or the commander in general starts and the general follows. Kesu is singing and enjoying the moment fully. Dancing and swinging in the tune of joy and intoxication. Tyagi is different. He is enjoying and singing along but he is not fully engrossed in the celebration. He is planning and conspiring something at the same time. He is saying that he has neither a sheet nor a blanket to cover himself from the coldness of the weather.

See how intelligently coldness is used here. The whole song is not an item number but the inner feelings of Langda Tyagi or Iago. He is angry, frustrated, and fully taken aback by the fact that the commander in general or Bahubali's post is given to Kesu/Casio and not him. He is fuming with fire of anger and is furious. The cold air that is present in the weather is a resonance of his numbness of emotions and he no longer feels any affection, loyalty, or any emotion towards any person he knows.

He starts his conspiracy by trapping Rajju/Roderigo and convincing him that he would unite him with Dolly/Desdemona. Then he goes on to make a plan to dethrone Kesu from his post.

Notice how the lines –*"Ja padosi ke chulhe se aag lai le"* coincide with what he is conspiring.

The next lines would just highlight what I said.

Beedi jalai le jigar se piya
Jigar maa badi aag hai
Beedi jalai le jigar se piya
Jigar maa badi aag hai
Dhuaan na nikari o lab se piya
Dhuaan na nikari o lab se piya
Je duniya badi thaag hai
Beedi jalai le jigar se piya
Jigar maa badi aag hai

Translation-

Light your cigarette from my bosom
There is a lot of fire in my bosom
Light your cigarette from my bosom
There is a lot of fire in my bosom
Don't let any smoke come out from your mouth
Don't let any smoke come out from your mouth
This world is like a thug
Light your cigarette from my bosom
There is a lot of fire in my bosom

These lines are the feelings of Langda Tyagi/ Iago. He is fuming with anger so much that he is unable to contain it or suppress it but he has to or he might even be robbed of the position he has now. "Dhuaan na nikari o lab se piya, Je duniya badi thaag hai"

After this, there is a repetition of the first paragraph and again, we see Tyagi saying something to Rajju. The conspiracy continues and the lines "**Ja padosi ke chulhe se aag lai le**" have a hidden meaning.

These lines and stanzas did give a sneak peek of his frustration and mental furiosity but the next paragraph reveals the pain and the feeling of helplessness and injustice he felt because of the decision that the leader took.

Na kasoor, na fatoor
Na kasoor, na fatoor
Bina jurm ke huzoor mar gayi, ho mar gayi
Aise ek din dupehri bulai liyo re
Baandh ghungru kachehri lagai liyo re
Bulai liyo re, bulai liyo re dupehri
Lagai liyo re, lagai liyo re kachehri
Angeethi chadai le jigar se piya
Jigar maa badi aag hai
Beedi jalai le jigar se piya
Jigar maa badi aag hai

Translation-

Neither was it a mistake, nor a defect
Neither was it a mistake, nor a defect
I got punished for no crime
One afternoon he called me just like that
In his court room I was asked to wear anklets
One afternoon he called me
In his court room
Ignite your brazier from my bosom
There is a lot of fire in my bosom
Light your cigarette from my bosom
There is a lot of fire in my bosom

His pain and the grief of the decision is shown clearly through the lines- "Na kasoor, na fatoor,Bina jurm ke huzoor mar gayi, ho mar gayi" His righteous post is snatched away from him without any of his faults, mistakes, or defects. He is punished without any reason. One day, he was called out in the court and he was bound (Ghungroo as a restrictive bondage on the leg) to follow the leader's orders. That was his(leader's) justice to me. The courtroom became unjust and the anger went to another level. This is so brilliantly justified by the next line that tells to light an Angithi or a brazier which is used for cooking. The fumes have become strong enough to light an angithi from a beedi. Pay attention to how Tyagi joins the dance exactly at the mention of Angeethi, as if he is the angeethi.

Na toh chakkuon ki dhaar, na darati na kataar
Na toh chakkuon ki dhaar, na darati na kataar
Aisa kaate ke daat ka nisaan chhod de
Yeh kataai toh koi bhi kisaan chhod de
Aise zalim ka chhod de makaan chhod de re Billo
Zalim ka chhod de makaan chhod de re
Aise zalim ka, O aise zalim ka
Aise zalim ka chhod de makaan chhod de

Translation-

Not a sharp knife, nor a sickle can match her
Not a sharp knife, nor a sickle can match her
Her love bites leave the marks of her teeth
No farmer has cutting tools like her
Billo, leave the house of such an oppressor
Leave the house of such an oppressor
Such an oppressor, such an oppressor
Leave the house of such an oppressor

Notice how this is the only paragraph which is started by Iago/ Tyagi. All the others are started either by Kesu/ Cassio or Billo/Bianca. Also, one must note that whatever is sung by Billo seems to be the emotional perception of Tyagi/Iago with regards to what he is suffering from and how his emotions are for the same. The injuries that the leader (Omi) has caused are no match to those puny ones of a knife or a sickle.

The bite leaves a mark. (Bite refers to the attack on him that has left a lifelong scar on him). These lines now show how badly he wants to quit the company of such an oppressor and make his own kingdom. (You can see how cunningly he is able to almost do that).

Na bulaya, na bataya
Na bulaya, na bataya
Hum mein neend se jagaya haai re
Aisa chauke lihaaf mein naseeb aa gaya
Woh elaichi khilai ke kareeb aa gaya
Koyla jalai le jigar se piya
Jigar maa aag hai

Translation-

Neither did he call me nor did he tell me
Neither did he call me nor did he tell me
He woke me up from my sleep
I was so surprised to see him in my quilt
He got closer to me by feeding me cardamom
Light the coal from my bosom
There is a lot of fire in my bosom

These lines are the description of how he woke him up from a deep slumber without any warnings. It is his good luck that he (Omkara) came close to him and came under his influence and also ate the cardamom (digesting the sweet talks and the manipulative ideas that he gave.) Coal is the final level of the burning as it leaves out no or the least amount of smoke. The mind has reached its highest threshold and there is no calming down now.

Also see how genius it is to end the song with a beedi actually burning and causing a fight lead by Kesu. Of course the visualization is of an escort dancing in a crowd and the people enjoying it but see how deeply woven the lyrics are. They are not simply there to make the dance number attractive or to objectify the escort that is dancing but to explain and poetically describe such a complex situation. The song becomes a masterpiece by everyone involved in it. Be it the ultra-expressive Deepak Dobriyal as Rajju, Tyagi as Saif, Kesu as Vivek or Billo as Bipasha. The lyrics are the fundamental base of this wonder and by no means one can ever doubt the lyrical storyteller in Gulzar. What is adding jewel to the crown is the seamless, ultra smooth, uber versatile singing of Sukhwinder Singh. If you did not notice, see how flawlessly he changes his pitch, tone, and singing a bit when he switches to singing for Saif Ali Khan from Vivek Oberoi. The voice becomes heavier and more intense. A voice that is waiting to be heard and waiting to do something drastic. And of course, the tune has hit the right chords with the super elegance of Sunidhi Chauhan who is just extraordinary in this song.

So, the next time one sees an item number, make sure that you also see the movie and keep in mind the makers of the song and the movie. You may find an ocean of brilliance and extraordinary art pieces hidden in it like this one!

8. Kabira – Yeh Jawani Hai Deewani

Recommended

Yeh Jawani Hai Deewani -

Yeh Jawani Hai Deewani is about Kabir, aka Bunny (Ranbir Kapoor) who is a person who wants to travel the world and experience all the cultures. He again meets Naina Talwar (Deepika Padukone) when he attends his best friend's wedding in Udaipur, Rajasthan. The movie revolves around the love of Bunny for Naina as well as his idea of never settling down in life.

Kabira becomes a song that encapsulates the feelings and indecisiveness of Bunny. Bunny is a person who has lived his life on his terms alone and cannot accept the idea of settling down in India with Naina who has found her life in Mumbai. The song shows how badly he wants to be with Naina and not let go of the love of his life but he is too reluctant to give up on his dream. Somewhere, the song also shows that Bunny is highly torn between the choice of his dream and his love. It is a difficult decision because he has lived alone all his life and now, he has to compromise on something. This baffles him and he sticks to what he knows until he realizes…

Kaisi teri khudgarzi
Na dhoop chune na chaanv
Kaise teri khudgarzi
Kisi thaur tike na paanv (x2)

Translation-

You are extremely selfish. You want both things and cannot let go of anything. Your will and wishes are everywhere and you cannot stay still in one place.

Analysis-

These lines show how Bunny cannot let go. He just cannot fathom the line that Naina has been always telling him- "Kitna bhi try kar lo Bunny, life mei kuch na kuch to miss hona hi hai." He has an extreme degree of Fear Of Missing Out (FOMO) and that builds on the indecisiveness. The song is a hard-hitting one because he knows his dilemma and he cannot come to terms with his choice. His idea has been to live a simple and uncomplicated life where he has only the goal of traveling but when he meets Naina, his ideas are challenged.

Ban liya apna paigambar
Tar liya saat samandar
Phir bhi sukha mann ke andar

Kyon rahegaya

Translation-

You have become your own messenger and travelled across the seven seas to live the life of a vagabond. However, you are still lonely, sad, and unsatisfied.

Analysis-

Bunny has lived his life and dream of travelling across the world and going and experiencing different cultures. However, he is still unfulfilled, lonely, and unhappy. This is a striking revelation to him as he thought that it would make him happy. It also shows how his life has been one of a lonely person. The closest people he has had are his friends, father, and Naina. He has lost his father and his friends are in touch with him. Naina is someone he needs to let go if he needs to continue the travel life. This is a striking point. It is also somewhere a resonance and repetition of how his father wanted him to do whatever he wanted to do but when his father needed him the most, he was not able to make it. This also haunts him and makes it more difficult to make a decision. He can live by himself but he would always be lonely or he can choose Naina and not travel. The liberal outlook of Naina and the freedom that Naina represents to him also becomes a difficult addition to make a choice.

Re Kabira maan jaa
Re Fakeera maan jaa
Aaja tujhko pukaarein teri parchhaiyan
Re Kabira maan ja
Re Fakeera maan ja
Aisa tu hai nirmohi kaisa harjaiya

Translation- *Oh Kabir, please listen. Your shadows and past are calling you. Why are you so detached and dishonest?*

Analysis- This is the point wherein internal turmoil of Bunny is presented in words. He is somewhere being dishonest to himself when he says that he is not so interested in living a life with someone at one place. He glances through the journeys and trips that he has taken but he feels a void. The void is something that he does not realize haunts him. It shakes his core and he is somewhere running away from it. This is perfectly resonated in words like parchaiyaan, (shadows) nirmohi (unattached) and Harjaiyaan (a betrayer).

Tooti chaarpaai wohi
Thandi purvaai rasta dekhe...
Doodhoon ki malaai wohi
Mitti ki suraahi rasta dekhe... ae... (x2)

Translation- The same broken cot and the cold breeze await you. The warm cream of fresh milk and the pot of mud witness your growth.

Analysis- Bunny has left everything to pursue the luxuries and the lifestyles of the world. However, it is the set of simple things that is awaiting him and somewhere, he is also craving them badly. He wants to enjoy the simple things of life. He wants to stay at one place with his loved ones that he can call his home. He has traveled a lot but does not have the peace and luxury of going home to a loved one. This is what this stanza describes and paints the pain beautifully.

Kaisi teri khudgarzi
Lab namak rame na misri
Kaisi teri khudgarzi
Tujhe preet purani bisri..
Mast maula, mast kalander
Tu hawa ka ek bavandar
Bujh ke yun andar hi andar
Kyon reh gaya...

Translation- *What is this selfishness of yours that you neither select the sweet nor the savory. How can you forget the age-old love? You are a breeze of cold air that can change and has massive energy and power but you have suppressed yourself and extinguished this power and energy. Why so?*

Analysis-

This is the epitome of Bunny's confusion and turmoil. He cannot decide what to do and is going ahead with what he previously decided. He has been alone and lonely all his life and got his company in travel and new countries. But now, he has found support and love which he cannot leave. As he leaves, he is getting shattered inside. Each step makes his heart heavier. He thinks that the opportunity and the life that he has lived while traveling is making him happy when he does not realize that he feels happy and at home only when he is with Naina. In fact, his situation is perfectly defined in the dialogue of Naina-

"Agar main do minute mei idhar aur rahi to mujhe tumse pyaar ho jayega" The more he stays with and around Naina, the more badly he falls in love. This is even more difficult than the first time because he had not actually felt the love and he was on a trip that made him happy. So, in a way, travel had gifted him the love of his life and somewhere, his all dreams had come true when Naina was present. If he leaves Naina now, there would be no coming back and he would probably never be able to be with Naina. Thus, he leaves with tears in his eyes while the turbulence gets worse with each step and never subsides until the end of the movie.

Re Kabira maan jaa
Re Fakeera maan jaa
Aaja tujhko pukaarein
Teri parchhaiyan
Re Kabira maan ja
Re Fakeera maan ja
Aisa tu hai nirmohi kaisa harjaiya.. aa..

Analysis- The repetition of the stanza becomes the ongoing echoes of this confusion in Bunny's mind. It never ceases and haunts him until he finally takes the decision at the end of the movie. Somewhere, he realizes how he and his actions are betraying his own heart and soul. He wants to correct it and live a life that is happier, cozier, and finer. Thus, he goes to Naina and somewhere settles down with the idea of only traveling in parts instead of always doing it.

Thus, the movie and the song beautifully represent the confusions and the dilemmas that we common folks face in life so often. It is this relatability that has made this movie so wonderful, impactful, and popular among everyone.

9. Kahin Door Jab- Anand

Anand -

Anand is a movie about a dying cancer patient who taught a doctor how to live life to the fullest and not be sucked into the whirlpool of grief and frustration. Anand won many hearts with its simple story and a great star cast. Kahin Door jab Din Dhal Jaye is a song from this movie that is written by Yogesh, sung by Mukesh, and composed by Salil Choudhary.

The song begins when Mrs. Kulkarani has bonded with Anand and they have become like brothers and sisters. Mrs. Kulkarni asks for his blessings when he just puts his hand on her cheek and as she goes away, says that he cannot even bless her saying "Tujhe meri umar lag jaaye" (May you live long) because he knows that his days are counted. This is the first glimpse of the internal turmoil that Anand goes through every day in his life but overcomes it to have a good life and a good impact on the people around him. The song becomes a fragment of his mind where you can see darkness hidden beneath the ever-joyful nature.

 The visuals of the song are simple yet sublime. There is sunset, sea waves, and trees- all symbols of nature that represent the circle of life and death. What takes birth on earth must die. The view of sunset becomes his main point of wonder which begins the song-

Kahin door jab din dhal jaye
Sanjh ki dulhan badan churaye
Chupke se aaye
Mere khayalon ke aangan mein
Koi sapno ke deep jalaye, deep jalaye
Kahin door jab din dhal jaye
Sanjh ki dulhan badan churaye
Chupke se aaye

Translation- Faraway when the sun sets,
The bride of dawn sneakily steps in,
Lightens a lamp of some bright dreams in my dark
abyss.

The first stanza itself is a deep ponder on life and death. Din dhalna can be said to be a parallel of dying and losing life. The bride of darkness becomes the death – albeit a beautiful one because she is dressed up like a bride and comes in sneakily with grace. She becomes the person who lights the lamp in the dark abyss of his life. This is quite metaphorical. There are two ways this can be seen-

One is the case when he sees that death will finally relieve him from the temporariness of life. The other perception being that he is finally united with his lover whom he left in Delhi. He has the flower in the song that resembles his lost love and his inability to confess his love because of his illness. He thinks that the union shall be complete when he dies and some of his dreams would come true after his death. The darkness of death shall be replaced by a bright hope of union in heaven.

Kabhi yoon hi jab hui bojhal saansein
Bhar aayi baithe baithe jab yoon hi aankhen
Kabhi yoon hi jab hui bojhal saansein
Bhar aayi baithe baithe jab yoon hi aankhen
Kabhi machal ke pyar se chal ke
Chhuye koi mujhe par nazar na aaye
Nazar na aaye

Translation-

When the breath becomes slow and burdensome and the eyes are full of tears, someone comes lovingly and touches my heart but I cannot see her.

Here, we see that he is talking about the phase just before his death. He is hopeful that he would feel and embrace the touch of the bride. He is describing how an invisible force shall sooth him when he is leaving the world. The transition from this world to heaven is described here. He would be full of tears for leaving such a life and leaving behind such a beautiful world. His breath would be heavy as he would be fighting with death to get just one more moment to cherish the beauty of the world. The breathing becomes a 'Boj' or a burden that struggles to mark its presence.

Kahin door jab din dhal jaye
Sanjh ki dulhan badan churaye
Chupke se aaye

Kahin toh yeh dil kabhi mil nahin paate
Kahin pe nikal aaye janamo ke naate
Kahin toh yeh dil kabhi mil nahin paate
Kahin pe nikal aaye janamo ke naate
Thami thi uljhan bairi apna mann
Apna hi hoke sahe dard paraye
Dard paraye

Translation- Somewhere, the hearts fail to meet while somewhere bonds of an eternity are made in a jiffy. There is a conflict in me which makes my heart hate me and becomes happy to take on the pain of others.

Here, Anand is clearly remembering his lover whom he could not unite with. He is sad about that yet compensates by saying that I have made better connections with many people here. This rationalization of him has made the heart of others and a part of him is distant from himself which finds solace in others' pain. This stanza explains a lot of things that we see in the movie. Anand is a person who is always happy and never shares his grief with others. Even when Bhaskar notices him singing this song and wants to ask about the grief, Anand refuses to share and divide his grief. When it comes to taking others' grief, he never fails. This quality of Anand is what makes him loved among all the people he comes across and he makes a good bond with everyone. Janamo ke naate or bonds of eternity are made by him through this way- whether it is sharing a moment of grief and making the mood light or making someone 'Murarilal' and befriending them for the lifetime.

Kahin door jab din dhal jaye
Sanjh ki dulhan badan churaye
Chupke se aaye

Dil jaane mere saare bhed yeh gehre
Ho gaye kaise mere sapne sunehre
Dil jaane mere saare bhed yeh gehre
Ho gaye kaise mere sapne sunehre
Yeh mere sapne yehi toh hai apne
Mujhse juda na honge inke yeh saaye
Inke yeh saaye

Translation- My heart knows all the differences and how my dreams turned into a rare gold that is hard to achieve. The dreams are what I have and that is what would stay with me even after my death. Even their shadow cannot be separated from him.

Death may separate him from life and the world but his dreams are his golden treasure. The heart knows all the differences and problems of the world but still, the dreams are the treasure that he always cherishes. The dreams have attained more value when he realizes that his time on earth is limited and there is not much he can do to achieve it. Hence, the dreams also become the hope that makes him think of a better afterlife and a lot of leisure time that he would have to make them come true. Even the shadows of the dreams cannot be separated from him or his mind.

Kahin door jab din dhal jaye
Sanjh ki dulhan badan churaye
Chupke se aaye
Mere khayalon ke aangan mein
Koi sapno ke deep jalaye, deep jalaye
Kahin door jab din dhal jaye
Sanjh ki dulhan badan churaye
Chupke se aaye

Translation-
Faraway when the sun sets,
The bride of dawn sneakily steps in,
Lightens a lamp of some bright dreams in my dark abyss.

Until death knocks his door of life, he shall be living and igniting the lamps of faith, hope, and optimism. This is what he does in each of his friend's life- be it evoking motherly and tender love in Nurse D'sa or making Bhaskar realize how negative and hopeless he has been. Just like how the sun sets and makes the moon brighter through its light, Anand slowly fades into the color of death but leaves his colors in Bhaskar. Bhaskar becomes the moon that reflects the light of the sun, Anand.

10. Khalasi

<u>Independent</u>

Khalasi is a song that celebrates the spirit and the courage of the sailors. It stands for the undying spirit, the unwavering faith and determination of the person, and the ability of the sailors to stand up and face any and every difficulty that comes to them. In fact, their attitude is stated in the fact that the very essence of being a human being is to face difficulty with open arms and come out stronger. Sung by Aditya Gadhvi, Achint, and the chorus of Coke Studio Bharat, the song beautifully embodies the gusto of living a life and facing any difficulty that might arise. While the song directly addresses the idea of being a sailor and a ship cruiser, it is essentially a metaphor for human beings who have faced enormous hardships throughout their lives and still stay strong with a smile and unwavering determination.

Interestingly, the song is also a parallel to a very famous folklore of Haji Kasam, a sailor who went on long journeys and he bravely tried to navigate a ship called Vijli. Sadly, he lost his life to Mother Nature's wrath but was the one who would stick by the ship and try his best to ensure that the ship goes through as safely as it can.

Another trivia is the fact that there was a play upon the folktale of Haji Kasam called Vijdi wherein Aditya Gadhvi was an integral part. He was the singer in this musical and used his voice and poetry to add supreme effects to his folktale.

Aditya Gadhvi is a famous folklore singer and poet of Gujarat who has sung many Gujarati songs and is lovingly known as Kaviraj by his admirers. He wears many hats with elan, be it singing, acting, or writing. He is also the writer of the song. Putting music to the song is Achint, the composer who gave Scam 1992 its iconic theme and is a supremely versatile composer whose potential can also be witnessed in one of the best movies of 2022- Monica, O My Darling. They have joined their hands to serve a beautiful song in the form of Khalasi through Coke Studio Bharat- an initiative to showcase the real Indian culture. Here is the song to refresh your memory-

The analysis and the meaning starts below-

[Intro]
Gotilo, tame gotilo gotilo gotilo
Gotilo, tame gotilo gotilo gotilo

Nathi je majhaama
Khaali vaavataa dhajaa maa
Evo haad no pravaasi gotilo (x2)

Meaning- Find. Go find a sailor who is not riding high on the waves of life and not flying the flag high on the mast.

Analysis- The song starts with a call or a challenging tone. A tone that celebrates the courage and the enthusiasm that the sailors hold. This start is repeated twice. Notice how it establishes the mood of the song and gives you a pumping feeling of being alive. The first stanza is just spoken by Aditya Gadhvi while the chorus joins him for the repetition. The repetition becomes a symbol of infusing the music in the song and making the folk sound come alive. It also emphasizes the spark of life. If we stretch this to the metaphor of human life, we are talking about human beings who never give up and are always ready to live a life that is full of difficulties. Even in the difficult times, the flag stays up and the valor is steady as a rock.

[Verse 1]
Kaanthethi jaa tu jaa, dariye
Dariye thi jaa tu jaa, taliye
Kaanthethi jaa tu jaa jaa

Gotilo, tame gotilo gotilo gotilo, ohho(X2)

Meaning- Go from shores to the seas and search wherever you want. Please, go and search!

[Pre-Chorus]
Ae vehva do, vehva do, vehva do jyan vahiye
Vehva do vehva do, vehva do
Revaado, revaado, revaado jyaan chhaiye
Revaado, revaado, revaado
Vehva do, vehva do, vehva do, have
Revaado, revaado, revaado, have

Meaning- let him flow and do not stop.

[Chorus]
Nathi je majhaama
Khaali vaavataa dhajaa maa
Evo haad no pravaasi gotilo

Evo kon chhe khalaasi mane kaidone
Enaa thaam ne thekaana mane daidone
Evo kon chhe khalaasi mane kaidone
Gotilo, tame gotilo gotilo gotilo (X2)

Meaning- Find a sailor who is not enjoying life. Find a traveler who is regretting their journey. Please find a sailor like that and tell me. Please tell me his address and village. Tell me who is such a person who does not love their life.

Analysis- A true sailor is omnipresent but you would not find a sailor who is not ready to face the challenge of the storm. A wayfarer whose will is shaken by the storms of life is impossible to find. Still, if you find them, do let me know. The writer of the song says that every human is faced by challenges. Sure, they do get upset and disappointed and hurt. But they never give up. The meaning of being a human is to be the traveler of a journey called life and face all the ups and downs. Every person does face them but no one gives in. The journey does not stop. From the narrowest of streams to the widest of oceans, the Khalasi faces them all with a smile.

[Verse 2]
Khevaiyaa, o khevaiyaa
Hambo re hai, hai, haiyaa
Niklijaa laine tu taari naiyaa
Hambo re, hai, hai
Hambo re hai, aye
Meaning- Seafarer, O Seafarer! Hail and heave! Pick up your oar and sail with your boat to sail the sea!

Analysis- This is an important verse. This one shows a deviation from the ongoing music and style. The voice changes and the music has a modern touch now. In a way, you see a journey. A journey when the sailor started sailing and now, when he has tested the waters. He is going on and there is no stopping him. Also, we see how the seafarer has embraced new ideas and new culture that has made him a better person. We see a hint of rock and pop music in this otherwise folk song. The music blends and so does the time and culture. This verse also proves to be a pivot that changes the direction of the song and the music in it.

[Pre-Chorus]
Ae vehva do, vehva do, vehva do jyan vahiye
Vehva do vehva do, vehva do
Revaado, revaado, revaado jyaan chhaiye
Revaado, revaado, revaado
Vehva do, vehva do, vehva do, ahi
Revaado, revaado, revaado, ahi
[Chorus]
Nathi je majhaama
Khaali vaavataa dhajaa maa
Evo haad no pravaasi gotilo

Evo kon chhe khalaasi mane kaidone
Enaa thaam ne thekaanaa mane daidone
Evo kon chhe khalaasi mane kaidone
Gotilo, tame gotilo gotilo gotilo
Evo kon chhe khalaasi mane kaidone
Enaa thaam ne thekaanaaane daidone

[Post-Chorus]
Are, jadelu na shodhe
Ane shodhelu na gote
Evo khaarvo khalaasi goti lo

Meaning- While the repetition of finding the sailor and letting him flow goes there is a new line that adds meaning to his journey. The seafarer never finds something that he already knows or he is already acquainted with. He is an explorer and he would find the unfound.

Analysis- The repetition plays an important role to show how the core of the Khalasi or the seafarer is the same but as he proceeds, his way and the route is never the same. The journey is the destination for the seafarer and he is an explorer who would venture into the unventured territories. Perhaps this is the perfect explanation of human nature. We humans love to explore and have a tendency to go on adventures. This is why we get up and go traveling. This is also why we do not go to the same places again and again and instead, explore the unheard and unknown.

This is also an important addition as this shows the journey. The navigator has witnessed so many events and now has grown. The hearts want something new. Also, the heart has imbibed and learnt so many things that it has become addicted to the idea of learning and the idea of exploring new things. There is no stopping to this and it would be fatal to stop. That is life and that is the essence of living.

[Verse 3]
Are, kinaaraa toh sthir ane salaamat hoy
Pan maanas ena maate nathi sarjaano
Arre kharvo khalasi toh ee kehvaay
Ke je fanidhar naag jeva dariya ni haame utre
Ane utarvu pade kaaranke…

Meaning- Shores are stable and steady. Humans are not made for these stable shores. A true sailor would be the one who would step into the sea which is a humungous snake like Kaliya, the venomous snake that Lord Krishna killed. And a mariner would venture into these storms because…

Kinaare to Khaali pade naani naani pagli ne
Naanaa eva sapnaa ni ret vaali dhagali ne
Tofaano taraap maare
Halesaao haanfi jaay
Toy jeni himmat
Ane haam nahi haanfe

Meaning- The shores would have tiny footprints which would be washed away in a jiffy. The storms are the true tests of their guts. It is the place where their courage does not dampen and dim.

Evo khaarvo khalaasi
Evo haadno pravaasi
Evo khaarvo khalaasi
Evo haadno pravaasi

Meaning- Find a true mariner and an adventurous traveler.

[Hook]
Gotilo, gotilo
Gotilo, gotilo
Gotilo, gotilo
Gotilo, gotilo
Potaanaa j dariyaamaa
Potaanij dubkithi
Jaatnu amulu moti lo

Meaning- Find him. Dive deep within yourself to find your worth and relish the values that you have!

[Outro]
Nathi je majhaama
Khaali vaavataa dhajaa maa
Evo haad no pravaasi gotilo
Ae, Gotilo, tame gotilo gotilo

Meaning- Find the sailor who is not high on life and does not wave the flag with rigor.

Analysis- As the mariner has had experiences and has shaped his life with cultures and lifestyles, he is now ready for the worst kind of challenges. Let it be in any form, be it the most horrific storm that is equivalent to the venomous giant snake like that of Kaliya, who was defeated by lord Krishna. It signifies how a human being is never afraid of facing difficulties. Additionally, there is also the expectation that life is not going to be always easy so a person is prepared, and when they are someone like a sailor who has faced challenges every now and then, life would seem empty without any challenges. It is a journey of facing the farce and coming out from each storm- stronger, sharper, and more experienced. Some scars would hurt, some scars would be the trophy of life that would celebrate the spirit and enthusiasm of living. And then, the sailor cannot be satisfied with staying put at the shore. He needs to venture into the humungous sea even when the stakes are high and the odds of survival are low. That is what drives him and makes him a true sailor. The spirits and the courage would be as high as possible and he would face anything, be it the wavering seas or the challenges of life. Hence, it is the life of a mariner. Go and find a mariner whose courage dampens because of a storm or one who stops hoisting his mast because of facing a wreck.

Thus, that was the analysis and interpretation of Khalasi from Coke Studio Bharat. It is a song that is a true fusion of Folklore, a bit of rock and rap. It is also a unique song which catapulted the Gujarati songs to popularity and gave it a new identity.

11. Lag Ja Gale- Woh Kaun Thi

<u>Spoiler</u>

Woh Kaun Thi-

Woh Kaun Thi is a suspense thriller that revolves around Dr. Anand who once gave a lift to a mysterious woman and ever since then, the woman appears to him and causes him to appear crazy. This movie is one of the most popular movies of the 60's and its songs have gained a cult status, especially the blockbuster 'Lag Ja Gale' which shall be analyzed here.

Lag ja gale comes when Dr. Anand has found the eerie resemblance and proof that her wife is the person whom he gave lift to. He works extra and avoids going home in order to avoid meeting her and does overtime in the hospital. Sandhya comes to the hospital and convinces him to go out in the open where they are alone and can spend time together. It is later revealed that it was not Sandhya who performed this act of seduction and convincing but her twin sister. The song would echo the parts that would affect both the sisters and become a convergence of how the two are a cause of madness for Dr. Anand, one with full knowledge of the deed while the other becoming a scapegoat in a trap.

Lag ja gale ke phir ye
 Haseen raat ho na ho
 Shaayad phir is janam mein
 Mulaqaat ho na ho

Translation-embrace me, we don't know
whether this beautiful night will
ever be there again or not.
 We don't know whether in this life
 whether we'd meet again or not.

The first stanza establishes several things for the film. It appears as if the woman is her wife wherein the people who have watched the film are informed that it is indeed her twin sister. This act of seduction is enough to make Dr. Anand go crazy and fall madly in love with her. This stanza also foreshadows death. The first instance of death is when Sandhya is forced to leave the house on Dr. Anand's order and the train meets an accident. This becomes the first instance of foreshadowing wherein we can see Sandhya's longing of his acceptance for her and finally unifying with her. The next element becomes the act of seduction by the twin sister to make him fall in the trap designed by his cousin brother. She becomes the instrument of execution and her meaning of phir yeh haseen raat ho na ho points to the idea of Dr. Anand proven to be a mentally challenged person and spending time in rehabilitation.

Ironically, this idea backfires to such an extent that Sandhya is saved whereas her twin sister dies in the process of saving the plan. This happens in the climax of the film but the song proves to be sowing the seed of distance and separation at various levels- physical, romantic, and spiritual.

Perhaps the most interesting thing about the song is how beautifully the instruments are streamlined with the two. Notice how the violin would play when the focus is on Dr. Anand. His conflict, confusion, and longing is perfectly embodied in the violin tune. He is extremely puzzled as to how this is happening so quickly and how Sandhya is present everywhere and knows everything. A part of his mind is convinced that it is Sandhya who is doing this act while a part is still confused as to how it is so complicated and simple at the same time. He wants to unearth the mystery and figure out what this is all about. Lastly, he also likes the woman and finds her extremely beautiful. He wants to give in to the feelings of love and attraction but he knows that this is no less than an act of mystery and if he gives in, he might fall in deep trouble.

This violin tune is romantic, slow, and carries grief in it. The feeling is neither perfectly pleasant nor perfectly sad. The violin is perfectly contrasted by the guitar and the xylophone notes that are played when

Sandhya sings. She is clear in her emotions and in her motive. There is no dual nature in her words but the emotions are hidden. She is appearing and thinking about something. This dual nature is contrasted with that of Anand's by the usage of multiple instruments as well as lyrics. Anand's simplicity becomes the violin whereas the layers of intention become the multiple instruments that are used in Sandhya's singing.

Humko mili hain aaj ye
Ghadiyaan naseeb se
 Jee bhar ke dekh leejiye
  Humko qareeb se

Translation -We have got these moments with much luck.
Take a good, close look at me.

Phir aap ke naseeb mein
Ye baat ho na ho
Shaayad phir is janam mein
Mulaqaat ho na ho

Translation - we don't know whether it's in your fate or not
to see this again...
We don't know whether in this life
whether we'd meet again or not.

There is a sense of foreshadowing and separation here again. However, this is also a challenge to Anand from the doppelganger. She is challenging him to have a closer look at her and convince himself that it is Sandhya that is present everywhere and that is the absolute truth. She also says that this is a golden opportunity and this shall not be repeated again. Another interesting thing is the danger that is there in the role of the doppelganger. She knows that if she gets caught, things can get messy and she might even be jailed for life. The idea of not being able to meet again is also reflected in the lines 'Shaayad phir is janam mein mulaqaat ho na ho'. The song becomes an ill omen and also a sign of how what appears shall not be what it is.

Paas aaiye ke hum nahin
Aayenge baar baar

Baahein gale mein Daal ke
Hum ro lein zaar zaar

Translation -
Come closer, I'll not come again and again.
Let me embrace you and cry my heart out.

Aankhon se phir ye pyaar ki
Barsaat ho na ho
Shaayad phir is janam mein
Mulaqaat ho na ho

Translation-
we don't know whether love would
shower ever again like this or not.
We don't know whether in this life
whether we'd meet again or not.

Lag jaa gale ke phir ye
Haseen raat ho na ho
Shaayad phir is janam mein
Mulaqaat ho na ho...

She says that she would not come again and again
which is contradictory to what happens in the movie.
She is omnipresent and like a ghost who has haunted
Anand. However, there is a sense of regret,
disappointment, and also grief that haunts Sandhya's
twin. She has never been loved and gotten a feeling

of acceptance. This absence has made her devoid of feelings and she has become the actor in the trap of Ramesh, Anand's cousin. Anand becomes the point of love that she always lacked in life in any form possible. Additionally, the lines 'baahein gale mein Daal ke hum ro lein zaar zaar' become the grief of Sandhya that she has been so unfortunate that her husband has not even accepted her. A hug would become her acceptance and she would finally be overjoyed with happiness and acceptance.

The idea of that moment being so precious and irreplaceable is presented in the next stanza. This goes in both the cases- the doppelganger would never become weak again and feel loved and Sandhya not feeling the highest form of joy that she would feel now if he accepts her. The tears become the symbol of unexpressed latent feelings that both the cases would realize. The visuals also play a significant role here when the twin sister goes closer to him but requests him to come closer. This is striking because she is pulling him in her trap and she only needs to ignite the trigger for him to come closer and become her victim. There are multiple emotions in her but she is actively doing the role of a seductress who has laid a trap for him and would finally frame him for something he is not.

Anand's conflict reaches its peak here when she is so close yet so far. She has been near to him but he has no understanding of her whatsoever. His steps that go closer to her only increase the distance. However, his conflict is temporarily resolved as he gives in to his attraction to her and embraces her. This is where the violin tune stops playing.

Thus, the song becomes a very important plot point that intensifies the mystery as well as adds depth to the character of Sandhya and her doppelganger. Dr. Anand becomes more and more puzzled and the song is a seed that grows into full madness because of which he becomes hospitalized. This song and the song 'Naina barse Rimjhim rimjhim' become the tools that haunt his mind and keep bothering him. It is easier to forget a talk or a conversation but a song becomes difficult to forget because of the musical arrangement and the rhythm that is in it. Naina barse Rimjhim becomes a repeating song that comes and haunts him while Lag Ja Gale embodies his defeat to the ideas and the trap of his cousin. He has fallen into it and now there is little he can do.

Lag Ja gale portrays this defeat beautifully by tracing his feelings from being a reluctant and resolute person not going towards the twin to a man who has become a victim of a trap and fallen into the hands of a trickster.

12. Mann Kasturi Re- Masaan

Spoilers

Masaan-

Masaan is a brilliant movie that touches upon various parts of the society and showcases two wonderful stories that eventually converge into a Sangam. The movie is highly symbolic and full of depth. Each of the songs plays an integral role in moving the story forward and adding narrative depth to the story.

Mann Kasturi re is one of those rare songs that has a sad tone but not the usual tone that we are used to hearing of some typical sad tunes accompanied by an ever-present Arijit Singh's voice. This song is oozing with poetry, philosophy, and depth. The lyrics are taken from the poem by Dushyant Kumar and the phrases are often similar to those of Kabir. This makes the song unique, spell-bounding, and in the truest sense, melancholic. There is a pain that you can feel. Not the one that you usually feel in sad songs of crying but a pain of regret, disappointment, and something being snatched away from you. You are not sad because of a romantic heartbreak but you are sad because the very root of your existence is snatched away. Now, let us get into an in-depth analysis of the same.

Mann kasturi jag dasturi
Baat hui naa puri re
Mann Kasturi

Translation-
The heart is like a deer and it never gets what it is looking for.

Here, see how the lyrics beautifully blend with the situation. Vicky Kaushal works at a crematory in Banaras. He is in love with a girl (Shweta Tripathi). However, one day he gets a body for cremation and while he is arranging for the cremation, his sight falls on the hand of the body. He discovers the ring that he gave to her. He is broken apart. A really blank and emotionless wave captures him. See how he sits. He is unable to even cry. The shock has transported him to a temporary death. He is numb. After some time, his numbness transforms into a fit of anger in which he throws away the ring. See how Baat hui na puri re is literal as well as metaphorical. He wanted to talk to her and wanted to share his life with her. It also means that the episode or story that they both had is incomplete. After that, he sits and you see him biting his hand. It is as if he is confirming that this is not some nightmare and the reality. Also notice how gradual and growing the emotions are. First, you see numbness. Then, anger replaces that numbness. The anger is then replaced by a reality check. In barely a minute's time, the song and the acting show a myriad of emotions and feelings. It is touching, complex and deep.

Khoje apni gandh na paawey
Chaadar ka paiband na paawey

After confirming all of this as reality, he realizes what he has done and jumps into the ocean to fetch the ring he has thrown. See how perfectly the lines *Khoje apni gandh na paawey Chaadar ka paiband na paawey* fit perfectly with the action. Vicky cannot seem to find the ring now and his fragrance of happiness. It seems that he has lost all of it and cannot find it even though he tries his best. Chaadar is a word used by Kabir to denote life and Paiband is patchwork. Vicky just cannot seem to heal and patch his life. His life is broken apart and there seems no patch that would take care of it.

Bikhrey-bikhrey chhand saa tahley
Dohon mein ye bandh na paawey
Naachey ho ke phirki lattu
Khojey apni ghoori re
Mann kasturi

He is shattered like a broken glass and nothing can bind him. Even philosophies of life and consolations by people don't seem to have any effect on him. He is dancing like a top without an axis. He is without balance and cannot find a pivot to spend his life on. See how beautifully the lines about pivot *Naachey ho ke phirki lattu Khojey apni ghoori re* blend with his stare at the flower. The flower seems to be the axis of his existence which is moving apart and he is totally helpless.

Paat na paya meetha paani
 Or-chhor ki doori re
 Mann kasturi

Translation-
Even the shore and water of ganges could not bridge the gap between him and his lover. His heart is like a deer, still finding its roots.

Although there is little to no lyrics now, the visuals continue to be profound. See how there is a transition in Vicky Kaushal. He is stuck with sadness and grief. He is so sad and aggrieved that he sits on the shore and it becomes the morning. See how the expression on his face has also changed now. The morning resembles hope and his grief has become an understanding now. When he sees the man praying, he realizes the cycle of life. What takes birth has to die. Then the visuals show him on a boat and he looking at the sky full of birds. The birds symbolize freedom of the soul from all worldly connections and bonds. Lastly, he goes and hugs his father. There is a tiny smile on his face. This shows how he has become grateful for who he has in life and wants to cherish them.

Slight deviation- You can skip this part if you want to.

An interesting take on this is the comparison to a theory known as the Kubler Ross model. Basically, it lists the five stages of grief when a person experiences a loss of a loved one. It includes

1. Denial (Vicky refuses to believe what happened and sits in a shock.)
2. Anger (He throwing the ring in the water)
3. Bargain (he trying to see if this is a nightmare and also his search for the lost ring. Notice how the ring becomes an embodiment of his lover. He once had it but now he has lost it and cannot find it)
4. Depression (his grief and numbness signified by him sitting on the shore for the full night)
5. Acceptance (The visuals of a person praying, the free birds, and hugging his dad for being grateful to him)

Back to analysis.

While the lyrics continue to be the Mukhda (the hook line) , the visuals show how he has moved on. He has applied for a job and he got through the interview.

Paat na paya meetha paani
Or-chhor ki doori re
Mann kasturi

See how perfectly the visuals are of the crematorium when the lines *paat na paya meetha paani* come. The dead and alive are way apart and no link or bridge can connect them. Additionally, see how moving on in life is literally parallel with him moving to Allahabad. However, it is important to note that even though he has moved on and carried on in his life, the sadness is alive.

Life goes on but the sadness remains for the longest of time. What hurts more is the things that are left incomplete.

References-

Varun Grover's lyrics explanation

Kubler Ross Model

13. O Sajni Re- Laapataa Ladies

<u>Recommended</u>

Laapataa Ladies-

Imagine an era where newlywed women are clad in sarees that cover their face. Laapataa Ladies is one of the movies where two newly wed women are exchanged because of confusion on the train. The wives are changed, and each try to find a way out to their desired destination. Phool, the wife of Deepak, is now on the station somewhere miles away from the house. Deepak is with a bride that is not his. He realizes this when they reach his home and the family asks the bride to lift the ghunghat. What follows is chaos, longing, desperation, escape, and self-discovery. The plot and the film are simple and straightforward but it touches your heart. Craftily written, perfectly acted, and supremely well executed, the movie becomes a vehicle of a message that is long due to be delivered and understood by the people.

Laapataa Ladies is one of the best movies I have watched in recent times and it is a must watch. Some theaters still have this and if you are late, you can catch up by watching this wonderful treat on Netflix.

O Sajni Re becomes the emblem of the love, longing, and the desperation that Deepak harbors as he longs to get reunited with his wife, Phool, who is miles away. The song starts with a simple memory of the sweet conversation that Deepak once had with Phool. Deepak tries to impress Phool with the little English he knows. These are some words in a sentence that are the most in the family of watchmen. Finally, he says a full sentence to impress her- I love you. The song starts with this sweet memory.

O Sajni Re
Kaise Kate Din Raat
Kaise Ho Tujhse Baat
Teri Yaad Satave Re

O Sajni Re
Kaise Kate Din Raat
Kaise Mile Tera Saath
Teri Yaad Teri Yaad Satave Re

Translation- O my beloved, how do I pass day and night when I cannot talk to you! Your memories linger in my head and make me restless. How do I pass my day and night when I long to meet you.

Analysis- This is the place where Deepak remembers her and all the memories that they have had together. The wedding rituals, the functions, the meetings, and the small moments that make her smile. However, he feels helpless. The helplessness has begun because it has been sometime since the event happened and the couple separated.

Kaise Ghane Re Badra Ghire
Teri Kami Ki Baarish Liye
Sailaab Jo Mere Seene Mein Hai
Koyi Bataye Yeh Kaise Thame
Tere Bina Ab Kaise Jiye

Translation- There are dark clouds of grief, sadness, and desperation ready to pour out their heart as they miss you. The tsunami in my heart evoked because of the separation needs to be stopped. How do I stop this? How do I live without you?

Analysis- Deepak has been trying to figure out and find out by checking out every place that is nearby. He waited and seeked the help of the police. There seems no hope. He is broken. In fact, there is a poignant scene where one of his friends suggests that something bad would have happened to her. Deepak is infuriated and physically abuses the friend just to badly break down later. He is shattered. He cannot contain this anxiety and pain. There are a lot of emotions to tackle. He is broken.

O Sajni Re
Kaise Kate Din Raat
Kaise Ho Tujhse Baat
Teri Yaad Satave Re

O Sajni Re
Kaise Kate Din Raat
Kaise Ho Tujhse Baat
Teri Yaad Teri Yaad Satave Re
O Sajni Re

Translation- O my beautiful lady, how do I spend day and night without you?? O my darling, how do I spend days without talking to you! Your memories make me long for you and I miss you so badly.

Analysis- We see that Deepak is now hanging on the last sliver of hope. He is breaking down more than ever before but he refuses to give up. He knows that Phool would never give up on him and so shall he. They would be united even if it is much later when a lot of time has passed. He has faith in her and their love. Hope and faith does not die.

We later see how the couple is reunited and their patience, perseverance, and hope has transformed into moments of happiness and union that they would cherish for a lifetime. Sajni re thus paints the love story of the couple- Deepak and Phool. It is a song that shows love, pain, longing, desperation, missing, and hope. Arijit Singh's voice combined with Ram Sampath's music and Prashant Pandey's lyrics give this movie a beautiful song that resounds with love, passion, longing, missing, and sadness.

14. Oo Antava Mava -Pushpa

<u>Independent</u>

Pushpa The rise-

The story is about Pushpa (played by Allu Arjun) who paves his way from being a coolie for a Red Sandalwood mafia to the top of the mafia. The song comes when Pushpa managed to safely transport tonnes of sandalwood from their godown without getting caught by police. The song is written by Chandrabose and the singer is Indravathi Chauhan

This song analysis is more of a lyric meaning and looking deeper into the song. It is diving deep into the lyrics analysis of Oo Antava and seeing the message behind it. There is little that the video adds to the analysis so if you feel like letting the video play and reading ahead, do that!

Also note that the song is available in Tamil, Malayalam, Kannada, and Hindi. I have chosen the Telugu version as it is the original language of the song. Here starts the song meaning of Oo Antava-

Koka Koka Koka Kadithey
Kora Koramantu Choosthaaru
Potti Potti Gowney Vesthey
Patti Patti Choosthaaru

Translation- It does not matter whether we wear a saree, or we wear short skirts. You stare at us women and always view us in a lecherous manner.

The song puts forward a perspective from the eyes of a female. It is a common fact that girls and women all over the world feel unsafe to venture out in a lonely street be it in the day or at night. They are started by men no matter what they wear.

Kokaa Kaadhu Gown U Kaadhu
Kattulona Emundhi
Mee Kallallone Antha Undi
Mee Maga Buddhey Vankara Buddhee

Translation – It does not matter what we wear. It is your eyes and thinking that is distorted.

This further elaborates how women are blamed and how it is a common practice to shame the victim in India. Victims of rape are often asked and blamed that they wore a certain type of clothes that "invited" rape. Little is done or acknowledged about the fact that the rapists saw the victim as their property and forgot basic human courtesy.

Oo Antava Mava
Oo Oo Antava Maava Hey
Oo Antava Mava
Oo Oo Antava Maava Hey

Translation – Will you agree to this, Men? Or will you disagree with this?

If there is a change that has to be brought about, it has to be from the men. The first step is to acknowledge the problem and know that it is very commonplace to forget respect and boundaries. Things like jokes and mockery are not okay.

Tella Tellaaguntey Okadu
Thallaakindhulowthaadu
Nalla Nallaaguntey Okadu
Allaarallari Chesthaadu

Translation – Men follow us and are ready to do anything for us if we are of a fair complexion. If our complexion is dark, we are teased and mocked.

Telupu Nalupu Kaadhu
Meeku Rangutho Paniyemundhee
Sandhu Dhorikindhante Saalu
Mee Maga Buddhey Vankara Buddhee

Translation- our complexion does not matter. You take your chance in any way that you get it.

Women are often victims of acid attacks and harassment on the streets. The attacks are done because they look beautiful and are so fair that someone likes them and asks them. When they are rejected, the rejected person throws acid on them thinking that would snatch away the beauty from the girl. Even similar things happen with girls who are not fair. There is no rationale behind anything. It is just pure lechery that one has and wants to satisfy that somehow.

Oo Antava Mava
Oo Oo Antava Maava
Haye! Oo Antava Mava
Oo Oo Antava Maava

Yetthu Yetthu Guntey Okadu
Yegiri Ganthulesthadu
Kurasa Kurasaagunte Okadu
Murisi Murisipothadu

Translation –
No matter how tall or short we are. Men always find joy in our figures and appearance.

Yetthu Kaadu Kurasaa Kaadu
Meeko Satyam Sebuthanu
Andhina Dhraakshe Theepu Meeku
Mee Maga Buddhey Vankara Buddhee

Translation-
Neither tall nor short matters. The grape that you reach is sweet enough and be happy with it. This is a reference to the story of the fox and sour grapes where the fox is unable to reach the grapes and considers them as sour with scorn. People fall into the trap of dishonesty and lust after other women while they forget their own wives at home.

Oo Antava Mava
Oo Oo Antava Maava
Haye! Oo Antava Mava
Oo Oo Antava Maava

Hey! Boddhu Boddhu Gunte Okadu
Muddhugunnaavantaadu
Sannaa Sannagunte Okadu
Saradaapadi Pothuntaadu

Translation –
We would get compliments such as cute if we are chubby and we would be run after if we are slender and beautiful.

Boddhu Kaadhu Sannam Kaadhu
Ompu Sompu Kaadandi
Ontiga Sikkaamante Saalu
Mee Maga Buddhey Vankara Buddhee

Translation -
The truth is that it is neither about chubbiness nor slenderness. It is about the evil ways of thinking that are present in the minds.

There is no escape from the shaming and the scrutiny of patriarchy that narrows down women to properties and objects of men. If we destroy this thinking, then we would see the beauty in each of us and also become better humans.

Oo Antava Mava
Oo Oo Antava Maava
Haye! Oo Antava Mava
Oo Oo Antava Maava Hey!
Una Yeh Unna...
Pedda Peddaa Manishilaaga
Okadu Phojulu Kodathaadu
Manchi Manchi Manasundantu
Okadu Neethulu Sebuthaadu

Translation-Some men would pretend that they are the greatest and the most harmless creatures on earth while some men would talk so sweetly and nicely that one would never think of them as wrong.

Manchi Kaadhu Seddaa Kaadhu
Anthaa Okate Jaathandi
Deepaalanni Aarpeshaaka
Uu Uu Uu Uu Deepaalanni Aarpesakaa
Andari Buddhi Vankara Buddhey

Translation – Neither goodness nor evilness that you show matters. It is your true face that comes out in the dark that reveals how good you are! The darkness reveals the mask of goodness that you wore to take advantage of.

So many people would pretend to be very nice and sweet and be like an angel to someone but as soon as they get a chance, they show their true face, which is the most horrific of them all! They are only nice to damage us at a vulnerable moment!

Oo Antava Mava
Oo Oo Antava Maava
Oo Antaame Paapa
Oo Oo Antama Papa

Translation – Will you agree to this, Men? Or will you disagree with this?
Men's reply- Yes, we do agree. Why would we disagree with the facts you have stated?

There is only a line that is sung by the chorus of men in the song. The reply acknowledges the facts and also states that this is a grim reality. The realization is striking. It is the first seed of change that is sown in the hope for a better future.

Thus, the song gives a very unique perspective. These types of songs often have a perspective that demeans and objectifies women. Item numbers are very common in movies across India. Seldom does it happen that a song conveys so much depth and meaning as Oo Antava has managed to. The only other song that I could think of is Beedi from Omkara. One may argue that the girl is dancing in both places, and it might not be very appropriate to that, especially if you belong to a Sanskari Family. However, we must also acknowledge the fact that dancers are a common profession and an occupation that many choose to be in. If it is their choice, then there is nothing wrong with it.

Here's to having better songs in the Indian Film Industry!

15. Pairon Ki Bediyaan- Udaan

Spoilers

Udaan

Udaan is a coming-of-age movie that tells the story of Rohan who wants to become a writer. After being expelled from his school, he is forced to live with his abusive father who treats him like a servant. Rohan's aspirations are shattered by his father and he is forced to work as a factory laborer against his will. The film traces his 'Udaan' (flight of freedom) from being a forced factory laborer under his abusive father to an independent person who leaves everything behind to pursue his dreams.

This song comes at the end of the movie and serves as an epilogue to the story. It is perfectly parallel to Kahaani- Aakhon ke parde which comes at the beginning of the movie and serves as a prologue to the story. Rohan has finally stood up for himself against his abusive father and ran away from his house. After spending the night at his supportive uncle's house, he has written a letter for his father and is determined to leave everything behind and start afresh.

The song starts when he is leaving Jimmy's (his uncle) house discreetly and Jimmy catches him doing so. Rohan also looks at Jimmy. Jimmy smiles and gives him an encouraging goodbye, to which Rohan replies happily. The song starts perfectly when the uncle waves him goodbye. This is the push that Rohan was always looking for. Jimmy has always been supportive of him and a major factor for him to pursue his dream. When he gets the small push, there begins a tale of hope and joy. A joy that is found in embracing the air of freedom. This joy and pure feeling are beautifully expressed by the pleasant and joyful Sitar chords. There are also notes being played on the keyboard. The keyboard notes are the symbol of the sadness that he has to leave his uncle too, who had been the springboard. This feeling resonated in Jimmy too.

Pairon ki bediyan khwaabon ko baandhe nahi re, kabhi nahi re
Mitti ki parton ko nanhe se ankur bhi cheere, dheere, dheere
Iraade hare bhare jinke seeno mein ghar kare
Woh dil ki sune kare, na darre, na darre

Translation-
The shackles on the legs can't lock the dreams
Even small seeds can dig through the layer of soil slowly
Those who have strong intentions in their heart
They never fear to listen and do what their heart

wants

As the lyrics start, we see a myriad of emotions on Jimmy's face. He expresses some momentary contemplation and retrospection. Then follows a very subtle mixture of sadness and happiness. He is sad because his beloved nephew is leaving him and he is happy because Rohan has the guts to pursue his heart and live a creative life that he always wanted to. This is perfectly symbolized by the fact that Jimmy is behind a grilled door that more or less resembles a cage. The symbol of cages and barbed wires have always been present in the film. There is also a feeling of freedom and imprisonment that Jimmy feels. It is like a prisoner who has successfully managed to free his inmate but has failed to free himself from the bounds of the prison. This feeling is perfectly expressed on Jimmy's face.

The lyrics are also perfectly synced with his feelings. As Rohan walks away, the camera focuses on Jimmy and the first line- *'Pairon ki bediyan khwaabon ko baandhe nahi re, kabhi nahi re'* plays. It is as if Jimmy is the artist who has always been restricted but his ultimate creation is his nephew who can fulfil his dream and live his life. His thoughts are never imprisoned. He might have been because of his orthodox family. He looks at his nephew walking away and enjoying the air of freedom.

*'Mitti ki parton ko nanhe se ankur bhi cheere, dheere,
dheere
Iraade hare bhare jinke seeno mein ghar kare
Woh dil ki sune kare, na darre, na darre'*

These lines are sung when Rohan is walking away. "Nanhe se Ankur" or a little seed is what is described in the metaphor. This is a parallel to Rohan. Rohan is young in age and his physical appearance is also smaller and comparatively timid to his father. Rohan has finally found the strength and courage to rebel against his father- "mitti ko parton" or a layer of soil.

This is a really brilliant and wonderfully done scene. Rohan first starts walking and then runs. There is a constant change of running and walking. This dynamic of walking and running is the expression of freedom and energy that he feels. Something that you would feel when you are overjoyed and overwhelmed with emotions so much so that it reflects in your body. Something that you just want to express and you cannot do so because you have no one to. The urge to reach someone and express your feelings makes you run. As he reaches near his home, he starts running. He does so when he is very near to the gate of his house. He reaches there and sees his younger brother Arjun waiting for 'Sir' (their father) to return.

Rohan and Arjun talk. As Rohan talks to Arjun and tells him that they shall be together away from Sir, the sitar notes are played but in a higher note. The hope that Rohan carried is now being resonated and amplified by Arjun. This is clearly visible in Arjun's eyes when he hears that they are leaving their torturous father. The happiness in eyes is felt by the note on the sitar, and in harmony, they create a flight of ecstasy that is felt by the brain and the body. This moment becomes the catharsis of both the characters and they are finally riding on the cloud of happiness after being drowned in the sea of fear and compulsion.

Subah ki kirno ko roke joh salakhein hai kahan
Joh khayalon pe pehre daale woh aankhen hai kahan
Par khulne ki deri hai parinde udke choomenge aasman, aasman, aasman

Translation-
A jail that can stop the morning sunlight doesn't exist
The eyes that can guard the thoughts don't exist
As soon as the wings open, the birds will fly and kiss the skies

These lines further strengthen the idea of freedom by comparing it with sunrays. As these lines are sung, Rohan looks at his home and the letter he has written. After a moment, he also removes the watch that his dad gave him. The watch is a mark of tradition and the lineage that his family followed. He is still unsure if the step he is taking is right or wrong. He thinks about it and finally puts the watch and the letter on the stone near the gate. As he puts it there, the lines repeat. The walls of his concrete home could not stop his free thought. The eyes of orthodoxy and tradition cannot guard his flight of fancy. He renounces that tradition by surrendering the symbol to the previous owner. He is no longer confined to the chains of his biological family and suppressed under the rock of a narrow mind. The watch and the letter are on the stone whereas he stares at the home with his head held high. Looks at the house for the last time and leaves with pride.

Aazaadiyan ... aazaadiyan
Maange na kabhi mile, mile, mile
Aazaadiyan ... aazaadiyan
Joh cheene wohi jee le, jee le, jee le

Translation-
Freedom ... freedom
You don't attain that by just asking
Freedom ... freedom

Those who snatch it are the ones who live it

As they both leave the house, there is the introduction of a number of instruments. The ongoing tune on the violin ascends to a higher pitch. Energetic music plays on drums and guitars. This harmony of music repeats for the time as the two boys walk to the gate. As they reach the gate, Aazadiyan is being sung. See how brilliantly the word is synced with the boys passing through the gate. They have achieved freedom. Their cage has an open gate and they are walking out from it with their heads held high. As they are walking ahead, the lyrics continue.

The boys are walking out and experiencing what it is like to be free. You cannot just attain freedom by asking for it. They have finally snatched it and are living it. Notice how freedom starts when they leave the house. The open roads and garden act as a strong contrast to the congested looking house and flat. The gate was also grilled.

Subah ki kirno ko roke joh salakhein hai kahan
Joh khayalon pe pehre daale woh aankhen hai kahan
Par khulne ki deri hai parinde udke choomenge aasman, aasman, aasman

Translation-
A jail that can stop the morning sunlight doesn't exist
The eyes that can guard the thoughts don't exist
As soon as the wings open, the birds will fly and kiss the skies

Rohan looks at sir going in an autorickshaw and stares at it until it reaches the house. We see that Rohan is a bit afraid and is unsure as to how sir would react. His action of swallowing the fear is visible. However, he is also confident enough to let it go and walk ahead leaving the fear behind with his father. There is a great amount of symbolism in this scene.

Firstly, the act of his father and him going in an opposite direction has been the crux of the movie. However, the act is still on but now they have changed paths. The conflict no longer exists and they have separated ways.

Secondly, the passing of the auto is symbolic of the time that the boys spent with their father. Rohan is a bit closer to the auto as compared to Arjun. They only spent a fraction of their life with their father. Sir did not take them ahead in life but like the rickshaw, took them in the opposite direction. They were growing up to slaves, physically and mentally instead of growing up to be thinking individuals. When they are walking on different paths, they are also leaving behind the regressive growth and substituting it with progressive growth that would make them independent, free, and thinking individuals who can make their own decisions.

Lastly, the timing of the lyrics and the visuals are extremely important and perfectly synchronized. As the first line- *'Subah ki kirano... hai kahan'* is sung, the camera shows the father sitting in the autorickshaw and going away. The auto has gone now and it resonates with where is the cage that limits the spread of morning sunrays! The second line- *'jo khayalo pe...hai kahan'* comes when the rickshaw is out of their sight and the father's vision is out of range to see these two kids. And the last line, *'par khulne ki...aasmaan, aasmaan...'* is in sync with Rohan swallowing his fear, looking ahead, and walking confidently and fearlessly. He has finally soared his wings and is ready to touch the sky.

The reading of the letter seems to have a little significance at the first glance but it holds multiple layers of narration. The letter is the outright challenge to the authority that Rohan faced. He is not only brave enough to let him know but also to state clearly what he is doing and he is taking Arjun with him. He has also threatened him that if he tries to find them, he would take legal actions. This is very important to the narrative as this is a rebellion of multiple things. He has overthrown his authority and threatened his existence. There is no sign of fear or submission.

This was what he said but a major part was the statement about love. Bhairav Singh never treated his children with love and always treated them like slaves. When the statement of love is read and Arjun goes with him, Rohan puts his hand forward for Arjun to hold. Previously, Rohan never treated Arjun properly until he was hospitalized. He was just another person for Rohan and Rohan never considered him his brother. This was perfectly symbolized in the scene where Arjun tries to hold Rohan's hand but Rohan refuses.

As they are going away from their father, Rohan puts forward his hand. This represents that he is no longer the son of an abusive father but himself. He has learned to go out of his father's wicked ideology which is not friendly with anyone. He has now left the lineage of traditions that suffocated people. Also, the holding of hands is a mark of love and friendship that the brothers have. The hand also becomes the support that neither Rohan nor Arjun had until now. They were left to themselves and were not supported.

Arjun was a major support when it came to listening to stories at the hospital. The hospital scene starts with Arjun engrossed in his story while others gradually joined. This is rare because children are not usually considered as 'givers or providers in any relations but here, Arjun acts as one and their bond is equal and complete.

Kahani khatam hai ya shuruvat hone ko hai, hone ko hai

Subah nayi hai yeh ya phir raat hone ko hai, hone ko hai

Kahani khatam hai ya shuruvat hone ko hai, hone ko hai

Subah nayi hai yeh ya phir raat hone ko hai, hone ko hai

Aane wala waqt dega panahein, panahein

Ya phir se milenge do raahein, do raahein

Khabar kya, kya pata

Translation-
Is the story ending or is it about to start
Is this a new morning or is the night about to start
Is the story ending or is it about to start
Is this a new morning or is the night about to start
The coming time will give me refuge

Or will I encounter the crossroads again
I don't know and I have no clue

As the letter ends with a congratulatory note of Bhairav's new wedding, he goes inside the flat and closes the door. Just then, *"Kahani khatam hai ya shuruvat hone ko hai, hone ko hai"* plays. Bhairav has gone inside while the boys are going outside. Both have a new beginning. The boys go ahead and now we are left with a question. Is this the beginning or the end of the story? Is it a new dawn or dusk to the day? The future is uncertain as it may be comforting or would place them in trouble. Who knows? They just need to walk ahead.

The song ends on a very open note. The Kahaani stanza is the epilogue here. There is no definite ending. The brothers might live a wonderful happy life ahead where Rohan finds success with his writing. Bhairav Singh may realize his mistakes and become a better person. The brothers might also end up living a miserable life on the roads and Rohan fails to succeed in writing. Bhairav Singh becomes more miserable and horrendously treats his new wife and daughter.

Khabar kya, kya pata?

16. Rishtey- Life in a Metro

<u>Recommended</u>

<u>Life in a Metro</u> -
Life in a Metro talks about the story of 9 people whose lives are interconnected. It talks about love, lust, sex, romance, marriage, and family. The film is simple in its plot and an integral part of the movie is the metro band that plays songs at various points in the film. The songs not only provide a musical touch to the movie but also move the story forward. They become stories inside a story. Rishtey becomes an introduction to the characters as well as the city. It can be said that the movie is about the city more than the characters. The title rightly justifies this point of view. The variety of emotions of the film are showcased in the songs from Rishtey to Kar Salaam.

Rishtey toh nahi rishton ki parchaiyan mile
Yeh kaisi bheed hai bas yahan tanhaiyan mile
Rishtey toh nahi rishton ki parchaiyan mile
Yeh kaisi bheed hai bas yahan tanhaiyan mile

Translation-
The city is so crowded and full of people yet there is a

haunting loneliness in it. When people go and try to find genuine connections, all they get is loneliness.

The introduction to the city of Mumbai is perfectly done through this song. As the movie starts, we are introduced to several characters- Shikha (Shilpa Shetty), Rahul (Sharman Joshi), Neha (Kangana Ranuat), Ranjit (Kay Kay Menon), Shruti (Konkana Sen Sharma), Monty (Irrfan), Shivani (Nafisa Ali) and Amol (Dharmendra). As we get connected to their lives, we realize that their lives are lonely and incomplete. The start of the song juxtaposes that feeling of these characters with the general feeling in the city. The city becomes a nest of loneliness where there are a lot of residents but no connections. It is like a silence that is full of noise. Notice how the full song is played in rain- a symbolic view of how each of them is crying internally and the rain becomes a cover for them. Also note the light tone- it is always dim to dark and not bright, personifying gloom and sadness.

Ek chhat ke tale ajnabi ho jaate hai rishtey
Bistar pe chaadaron se chup so jaate hai rishtey
Ek chhat ke tale ajnabi ho jaate hai rishtey
Bistar pe chaadaron se chup so jaate hai rishtey
Dhoonde se bhi in mein nahi darmaiyan mile
Yeh kaisi bheed bas yahan tanhaiyan mile

Translation-
Relationships fade away even though people live under the same roof. They get lost in the blankets on the bed. Even when people share the same bed, there

is no connection or relation left between them. When a person tries to find the connection that they might rekindle, they find nothing. It is a crowd of loneliness.

This stanza of the song paints the picture of Shikha's and Ranjit's story. They are both married and have a daughter. However, they are always fighting and in order to prevent their fights, they need to throw parties and call people at their house to have company and not get into fights. They are strangers who share the same roof. There is no love between them, and they are together out of compulsion and not because they love each other. Even when they share a bed, it feels as if they are forced to sleep there, and the compulsion is so strong that they can neither go away nor come closer. This dilemma is perfectly encapsulated in the song.

Jisko bhi dekhiye woh adhoora sa hai yahan
Jaise kahin ho aur woh aadha rakha hua
Jisko bhi dekhiye woh adhoora sa hai yahan
Jaise kahin ho aur woh aadha rakha hua
Ho jab jahan jude wahin judaiyan mile
Yeh kaisi bheed bas yahan tanhaiyan mile

Translation- Everyone here is incomplete here as if their better half is kept somewhere. When the incomplete parts meet, there is a separation that is worse than being lonely. This city is a crowd of lonely strangers.

This stanza becomes the portrait of Rahul's life and Shruti's life. They both live alone, and they are in search of love. They are not only without love but without any other close connection. This is a striking contrast to the pair of Shikha and Ranjit. They both have each other but the connection has faded. Rahul and Shruti have never found a connection in the first place. In fact, a closer look at Rahul's situation reveals many more complications in his life. Rahul has literally no one whom he can call a friend. He loves Neha but Neha rarely looks at him. He has a house, but he gives them to his bosses at night in exchange for a promotion recommendation. This has made his life a mere commercial exchange where everyone who interacts with him is either a customer of his call center or a boss who wants to use his house at night for sexual activities. Later, when he tries to connect with Neha and takes a step forward, he is lashed out by realizing that she is having an affair with his boss and has used his house for the night. This is where the line *'Ho jab jahan jude wahin judaiyan mile'* is perfectly personified.

Shruti is better when it comes to having someone in life. Shikha is her sister and Shruti shares the flat with Neha. However, when she finally falls in love, she is betrayed by her lover. *'Ho jab jahan jude wahin judaiyan mile'* also becomes a point of foreshadowing for Rahul and Shruti who are lonely now without love but become heartbroken and alone after finding love.

Rishtey toh nahi rishton ki parchaiyan mile
Yeh kaisi bheed hai bas yahan tanhaiyan mile
Rishtey toh nahi rishton ki parchaiyan mile
Yeh kaisi bheed hai bas yahan tanhaiyan mile

If the city is full of loneliness, you need to learn how to live with it. You would not find strong connections or relationships, but you would find glimpses and trailers of what a good relationship can be, and you must be either happy with it and live a positive life or sulk and be sad about the absence of someone whom you can share a good bond with. Remember the popular Akbar- Birbal story where a person survived a cold night in cold water just by looking at a lamp? The shadows of bonds are that lamp which people look at and survive their lives of loneliness.

17. Shauq- Qala

Spoilers

Qala-

Qala is a movie that haunts and affects the viewer deeply. It's a story about a girl who is born to an acclaimed singer couple. She tries to become a successful singer and the journey is filled with struggle, envy, and tragedy.

Please note- POTENTIAL SPOILERS

Shauq is a song that becomes the pinnacle of competition and ignorance for Qala. It is sung when the four of them- Qala, her mother, Jagan, and Chandan Sanyal. They are on a boat in the middle of the river when Sanyal starts singing this song which is one of his creations. Jagan joins Sanyal and when Qala tries to do so, she is stopped by her mother which shows the neglect and hatred that her mother carries toward her. What she does next changes her life and conscience.Let us look at the song in detail but before that, here is the video that you should watch to refresh your memory.

Bikharney ka mujhko shauq hai bada
Sameitega mujhko tu bata zara (x2)

Translation -I have a fondness for breaking apart and becoming a mess,
Please tell me this, will you pull me together?

This paragraph becomes the starting line for the song. The song is a metaphor for Qala and her life. Her life is a mess and no matter how many times she tries to put it together, it falls apart and entangles itself. Although these lines are sung by Sanyal Sahab, they are the tale of Qala who is dying to make a mark in the world and more importantly, get her mother's validation! It is also a plea to her mother to please help me to structure and organize my life. It is a mess because I do not know what to do and your absence is just making it worse than ever.

Doob-ti hai tujh mein aaj meri kashti
Guftagu mein utri baat... (female)

Ho, doobti hai tujh mein aaj meri kashti
Guftagu mein utri baat ki tarah (male)

Translation- My boats sink in your seas and the small talks lead to deep conversation.

The use of voices and the visualization is strikingly painful as well as symbolic. As soon as Qala starts singing, her mother stops her, and she encourages Jagan to continue. The shift is a representation of the mother's support. Qala's birth is considered a bad omen for Urmila (her mother) as that led to the death of his twin brother. She always saw Qala as a burden and whenever Qala tried to do anything, it was never enough for Urmila. However, Urmila sees that Qala is willing to work on singing and pushes her to learn it. Her treatment is always cruel and inhumane, but she still pays attention to her. When Urmila discovers Jagan, she sees her dead son in him. The minor amount of attention that Qala used to get is now diverted to Jagan and she is devoid of the bare minimum which was present before. In fact, the point at which Qala is stopped is "Baat", a symbol of how her words are never allowed to complete or even given a chance to be spoken.

When Jagan completes this stanza, Urmila is spellbound and continues to enjoy it. Urmila goes and flirts with Sanyal Sahab with the intention to convince him to give him a chance to Jagan by any means.

Ho, dekh ke tujhey hi raat ki hawa ne
Saans thaam li hai haath ke tarah Haaye
Ki aankhon mein teri raat ki nadi
Yeh baazi to haari hai sau feesadi

Translation- the night has held its breath after seeing you as if a person is holding a hand tightly, there is a river of the night in your eyes and oh, I have definitely lost this game.

Analysis- These lines work as a double metaphor. One is the simple flirting that Urmila and Sanyal are into, and the other is the dark side that Qala is experiencing. Night can be a symbol of romance and the moon, which is applicable to Sanyal and Urmila, but it is also a metaphor for darkness. The darkness engulfed Qala after she was stopped by her mother. It is as if her own hand has choked her, and she feels an extreme amount of pain. She witnesses a stillness and stoic attitude towards existence and efforts in the eyes of the mother and she feels that she has lost everything. The diversion of the love and affection from her to Jagan has been shattering for Qala and she feels that she has lost everything in life which is also why she takes such a drastic step to get the attention and fame that her mother wanted for Jagan.

Ho, uth gaye kadam toh

Aankh jhuk rahi hai

Jaisey koyi gehri baat ho yahaan

Ho, kho rahey hain dono ek doosrey mein

Jaisey sardiyon ki shaam mein dhuan haaye

Yeh paani bhi tera aaina hua

Sitaron mein tujhko hai gina hua

Translation- I take my steps towards you with my eyes looking down. There is a deep secret that is being held. We are merging into one another like the smoke merges with the fog in winter. This water is your mirror and I count you in the stars.

This can be said to be the turning point in Qala's mind. She is determined to get rid of Jagan and take some drastic steps to retrieve her position. This corresponds with the flirting of Urmila and Sanyal which can be seen as simple metaphors for flattery and poetry to get closer. Qala tries to befriend Jagan and lure him into the cold. When her mother spots that the apple of her eyes has caught cold, she asks Qala to serve her a remedy. Now, Qala is taking a step towards Jagan with steps that are long, but she is hiding a deep secret. As Qala does this deed, she takes the place of Jagan and manages to achieve what he was supposed to as per her mother. See how that merges with "kho rahey hai dono…sardiyon mein dhua." They have become the same thing- that is the achievement that the mother wanted. Also, the ghost of Jagan never leaves Qala, and it has become a part of her. The guilt has manifested into a connection that helps and destroys her. The most poetic and perfect line here is about water becoming the mirror. It is the first evidence that Qala has decided to do something drastic and harmful to get attention. This becomes the seed of the conscience that stares in her soul and eventually grows to become the tree that haunts her until she overcomes that. *'Sitaron mein tujhko hai gina hua'* . Just look at the depth this line displays. It is a twofold shot of being a star- one who is extremely popular and famous that people are crazy about them and the other being as someone who has died and become a star. The couplet becomes a prediction of the futures that Qala has. One in which she becomes the celebrity that she desired to be with fame and popularity and the other, becoming the star in the sky because her conscience keeps haunting her until she finally commits suicide.

Bikharney ka mujhko shauq hai bada
Sameitega mujhko tu bata zara

The last couplet also becomes a plea and a dying request of Qala. All she wanted was the attention of her mother and if the mother had paid attention in the last few days, she could have helped her and avoided her suicide. The guilt and the ignorance kept growing on her until she could see nothing. Also notice how the last song she sings has images of snow, the tree, and unbearable coldness. A location is a snow place- snow and cold being the symbol of the absence of warmth in her life. No one but Majrooh offered her warmth. When the last tinder of warmth that she used to get from her mother is extinguished, she succumbs to the coldness and dies of loneliness, guilt, and ignorance.

Thus, the brilliance of a team as brilliant as that of Qala- singers Swanand Kirkire and Shahid Mallya along with Sireesha Bhagatuwala, filmmaker Anvita Dutt, Lyricist Varun Grover, actors- Swastika Mukherjee, Tripti Dimri, Babil Khan, and Samir Kocchar. Qala is indeed a film that has touched many aspects and worked as a masterpiece. Glad to have such masterpieces in Bollywood

18. Yeh Tara Wo Tara- Swades

<u>Independent</u>

Swades-

Swades is a simple story of a man who returns to his native country India from America in order to meet his nanny and convince her to come back with him to America. The film traces the emotional journey of Mohan (Shah Rukh Khan) who initially misses his Nanny who is equivalent to his mother for her longing to be in his native land and serve the village and his country. This simple plot is met with a beautiful execution in Swades.

Mohan and the villagers have gathered to watch a movie and they are watching 'Yaadon ki Baarat' when there is a problem with the projector. Mohan takes it on him to entertain the upset children who were keenly watching the movie. He starts with showing a constellation that makes a plough (Also called Big Deeper, a part of the Ursa major). After grabbing everyone's attention and citing an example of stars, he starts the song that is about stars.

Aye hey ... aye hey
O ho ho o ... o o o

Yeh tara woh tara har tara
Yeh tara woh tara har tara
Dekho jise bhi lage pyara
Yeh tara woh tara har tara
Yeh sab saath mein
Joh hai raat mein
Toh jagmagaya aasman sara
Yeh sab saath mein
Joh hai raat mein
Toh jagmagaya aasman sara
Jagmag taare
Do tare, nau tare, sau tare
Jagmag sare
Har tara hai sharara

Translation-

This star, that star, every star
This star, that star, every star
Whichever one you see looks lovely
This star, that star, every star
When they all come together
In the night
Then the whole sky shimmers
When they all come together
In the night
Then the whole sky shimmers
The shining stars
Two stars, nine stars, hundred stars
The shining stars

Each star is a separate spark

Mohan shows the beauty of the stars and sings this song. The start of the song is a straightforward and direct message to the audience- the villagers. He is talking about how each star is beautiful, but the night only looks amazing when all of them come together and take their places. After they are in their places, there is no limit to what a collection of stars can form. This is a subtle message as to what he is going to convey through his song. The idea of unity is filled in the heads of the villagers who are reluctant to mingle with people belonging to other castes or religions. After singing the song, he also shows the constellations and the close up of the stars through his telescope.

This action of showing the stars and talking about the stars lays the perfect base for what message he wants to convey. He does not want to address the issue directly because he knows that it would not be of any use, especially when he has tried convincing people to send their kids to school but the ideologies are very different.

Pay attention to the music that accompanies the lyrics. There is a note on the Indian string instrument that keeps repeating. The instrument is very rustic and rural and signifies proper Indian culture. The repetition and the use of that instrument is present throughout the song. The notes sound as if they are the start of something that is going to change a lot of things. It also adds a ray of hope to the convincing vocals.

Tumne dekhi hai dhanak toh
Bolo rang kitne hai
Saat rang kehne ko
Phir bhi sang kitne hai
Samjho sabse pehle toh
Rang hote akele toh
Indradhanush banta hi nahi
Ek na hum ho paye toh
Anyay se ladne ko
Hogi koi janta hi nahi
Phir na kehna nirbal hai kyun haara
Hmmm hmmm hmmm ... tara tara

Translation-

If you've seen a rainbow
Tell me how many colours are there
There are seven colours to speak of
But they're so closely associated
First understand this
If these colours were separate
A rainbow would have never formed
If we don't manage to unite
To fight against the injustice
There won't be any people
Then don't say why did the weak lose
Hmmm hmmm hmmm ... star, star

As he has already sowed a seed of his message to the audience, he now further elaborates with another example- this time of a rainbow. A rainbow appears to have nine colours but they are so indistinguishable that you cannot pinpoint the point of difference. The gradual shift makes them beautiful. If the colors were separate, they would not have pleased the eye with a beautiful rainbow. This is how humankind should be-united to fight against injustice in society. If this does not happen, then one should not blame as to why they are losing.

This is also a path to make them realize their own flaws. Throughout the movie, the villagers would often play the blame game and never accept their own mistakes. The perfect depiction of this is when the government official comes to the panchayat and asks as to what happened to the electric poles and the villagers would blame one or the other for stealing the electricity. The idea of blaming the government and becoming an inactive part of the system is perfectly highlighted here. Also, they need to be united amongst themselves in order to achieve and bring about a change in society and their own village. If they do not do this and make an attempt to change, then there is no point in saying that we are weak, and the government does not help us.

A very significant part of the song is how he engages each and every one from the audience. He becomes the ultimate performer who does not simply stay at a place and give a sermon but covers as much ground as possible. This ensures that his audience connects with him at a deeper level. The most striking thing in the song is the usage of the curtain. The curtain is the division between the upper caste people of the village and the lower caste of the village. While he is in one part of the ground, the other can only see his shadow and the curtain blocks his real view. He would go from one part to another and keep changing his side so that he not only achieves a sense of equality and connection with all the people in the village but also gives each other the idea as to how the other feels when they are deprived of the full view. When he goes and interacts with the upper caste section of the people, the lower caste can only see the shadows. This was the case even when the movie was playing. The lower caste section was shown the inverse image of the film, and the curtain becomes the subtle yet evident symbol of discrimination.

However, Mohan realizes this injustice and he not only goes to the other side but also shows the upper caste section as to how it is to see the incomplete or flawed picture. The shadow play becomes a very important part of the song and beautifully creates a sense of empathy in everyone, including the movie viewers.

The music in this part of the song is accompanied by subtle yet significant flute notes. The flute becomes the perfect resonance of the hope, grief, and the limitless potential that the villagers have to succeed in life. The beauty of flute is its dual nature of how it can act as a soothing and peaceful instrument that elevates your mood and it can also act as a symbol of sadness and grief. This duality is perfectly explored here. It showcases how beautiful their lives can be if they come together but they are stuck in the turmoil of division and blame game that hinders their growth and development.

Yeh tara woh tara har tara
Yeh tara woh tara har tara
Yeh tara woh tara har tara
Dekho jise bhi lage pyara
Yeh sab saath mein
Joh hai raat mein
Toh jagmagaya aasman sara
Jagmag taare
Do tare, nau tare, sau tare
Jagmag sare
Har tara hai sharara

This repetition of the lyrics does multiple things at once. It not only reinforces his message but also shows some striking visuals that are full of symbolism. As he sings this, the first thing he does is to switch sides in quick succession. This causes a movement and also creates a situation where the attention is dynamic and troublesome. This small act is the perfect representation of how the curtain becomes the border that is creating problems and when the two sides are not able to see each other, they lack trust and there is a sense of animosity amongst each other. As he goes to the side of the potters, farmers, and ironsmiths, he includes them in the interaction again and never makes them feel isolated or excluded. The curtain is removed as he is dancing. This symbolic removal of differences creates a drastic change of emotions and feelings that range from subdued anger to fear and sheer happiness.

Again, we hear the flute now. This time, the flute is the prominent instrument being played which takes the center stage with the rustic instrument notes. This piece on flute adds up to the already established subtle flute notes played before. While the earlier ones were a symbol of potential and hope, these become the symbol of action, purity, and grief. These notes become the perfect carrier of fear and hope. We see how Gita is moved. She is full of fear, love, and she is touched by the action of Mohan. However, she is also afraid of the reaction that the villagers would give to the action of Mohan. She goes away from her place and stands far away so as to hide her tears and emotional reaction from Mohan.

The flute notes play on as Mohan mixes the children. The notes on the flute then become the sound of innocence and purity as the children mix up and they break age-old traditions of caste differences. The sweetness becomes a message of how sometimes breaking free is the best thing to do and makes a person feel more human than ever. The flute note also represents the myriads of emotions that the villagers show- some eyes are full of hope and happiness, some of subdued anger, some confused as to how can this even happen, and some so happy that their dreams would finally come true and they would break free from the strangles of an age-old tradition.

Boond boond milne se
Banta ek dariya hai
Boond boond sagar hai
Varna yeh sagar kya hai
Samjho is paheli ko
Boond ho akeli toh
Ek boond jaise kuch bhi nahi
Hum auron ko chhodein toh
Mooh sabse hi modhein toh
Tanha reh na jaye dekho hum kahin
Kyun na bane milke hum dhaara
Hmmm hmmm hmmm ... tara tara

Translation

When many drops unite
Then a river is formed
Every drop makes up the sea
Otherwise, this sea is nothing
Try to understand this riddle
If a drop is alone
Then the single drop is nothing
If we leave others
If we turn away from everyone

Then we will be all alone
Why don't we unite and form a current?
Hmmm hmmm hmmm ... star, star

The first two stanzas were the idea of unifying people, but this stanza not only conveys the message but also makes it a reality. The act of unifying the children and erasing the differences between them is perfectly done in front of the villagers. Mohan then goes to the Sarpanch community and explains the complexity of their thoughts. They think that the caste differences are the gift of tradition and upholding them is the way to progress. However, Mohan debunks this misunderstanding that creating differences will only result in isolation of everyone and then instead of a village or a community, there would be a group of disconnected people in a village. He goes to each of them and conveys this personally to them. The line *'Hum auron ko chhodein toh Mooh sabse hi modhein toh'* comes exactly when he goes to the Panch Munnishwer who is very unhappy with his ideologies and does not agree to the idea of unification and believes in continuing the old traditions. Only unification will help them to progress and have a stronghold in whatever they want to do in life.

Nivaraan and Melaram are also the perfect example of how he has executed what he preaches. Both are from different castes and they three gel in well together and do everything together. After he completes singing his part, Chiku comes forward and sings the chorus part.

Yeh tara woh tara har tara
Yeh tara woh tara har tara
Dekho jise bhi lage pyara
Yeh tara woh tara har tara
Yeh sab saath mein
Joh hai raat mein
Toh jagmagaya aasman sara
Jagmag taare
Do tare, nau tare, sau tare
Jagmag sare
Har tara hai sharara

This time, the message has reached a set of people, and it has already been applied. The kids have happily accepted this learning and are happy to dance to the newfound tunes of the joy of unity. They become the hope and the ideology of a better future. This is not only applicable to their success but also to the well-being and the growth of the village and the society. Chiku becomes the face and the representation of all the children, and he dances and sings to the tunes of joy. The stars have aligned in his favor, and he is happy to celebrate the moment.

Aye hey ... aye hey
O ho ho o ... o o o

This humming repeats to reach a sense of direction. The first humming and the half of the song is beautifully conveyed to the children, and they are in sync with what Mohan is saying. The children are singing his song and half of his work is done but the tougher one is still left. This humming becomes the symbolic call to the elders of the village. Even the children are dancing around the Sarpanch, symbolizing how they are seeing the future and the hope of the village being happy and joyous by coming out of the whirlwind of discrimination.

The music here is exceptionally well done. There are a number of instruments being played and the song finally achieves a dance worthy music on which the kids dance around the Sarpanch. The variety of instruments coming together signifies the unity and the bond that the kids have already established amongst them. This joy is perfectly resonated in the tabla beats that the kids dance on. They are celebrating a newfound freedom of having to make friends without being taunted for the choices. The joyous tabla beats are then accompanied by a strong violin tune that is the symbol of the conflict and anger that would have been in the minds of the Sarpanch committee. However, Mohan manages to explain and cool down the matter before it can even reach its peak and explode. He then tells them the following-

Joh kisaan hal sambhale
Dharti sona hi ughaye
Joh gavala gaiyan pale
Doodh ki nadi bahaye
Joh lohar loha dhaale
Har auzar dhal jaaye
Mitti joh kumhaar utha le
Mitti pyala ban jaaye
Sab yeh roop hai mehnat ke
Kuch karne ki chahat ke
Kisi ka kisi se koi bair nahi
Sabke ek hi sapne hai
Socho toh sab apne hai
Koi bhi kisi se yahan gair nahi
Seedhi baat hai samjho yaara
Hmmm hmmm hmmm ... tara tara

Translation-
A farmer who ploughs the land
Brings forth gold from the earth
A cowherd who raises cattle
Will flow rivers of milk
A blacksmith who shapes the iron
Every tool of his shines
A potter who shapes the clay
The clay becomes a pot for him
These are all faces of hard work
And a desire to do something
No one has enmity with anyone else
Everyone has the same dreams
If you think then everyone is ours

No one is a stranger to anyone
My friend, it's very easy to understand
Hmmm hmmm hmmm ... star, star

Mohan goes to each of the Sarpanch and explains to them how they contribute to society. His explanation is publicly addressed to them, meaning that he acknowledges their efforts and also states their value to society. However, he does it with each member of the community. He acknowledges the blacksmiths and the potters too. This is yet another execution of equality. He shows that they are highly interdependent and if they do not come over their differences, they would end up creating a world where they are deprived of each other's skills and would suffer in life. There is no difference or animosity amongst the producers. Each of them uses their skills to give the best output. Everyone wants to live a good and comfortable life and there is no reason as to why one would hinder another's growth. Hence, it is a very simple thing to understand, and they should acknowledge each other's work and not dismiss them just because their line of work is different from what they do.

There is a flute note exactly in the middle of the part when he goes from the side where the Sarpanch Committee is sitting to the side where the potters and blacksmiths are sitting. This is an exquisitely sweet and sad tune. They all have a lot in common and they are highly interdependent with each other, but they never actually recognize or acknowledge this fact. This has created the differences and has allowed the caste system to hinder their growth and success. The flute notes become this sadness of the enormous potential they have had and not utilized until now. It also becomes the symbol of how this is a good time to remove the differences and go ahead to eliminate them to finally utilize their potential. The duality of the flute becomes the duality of the emotions that Mohan feels and so does Dadaji, on whom the shot is picturized.

Also note how perfectly the flute comes in transition. It embodies the division and the sadness that the division has brought in them. The division that has also made the children suffer as it deprives them of basic education and the path to growth. This is then juxtaposed by the joyous tabla notes again which signify hope for a better future and the progress from a rather dull and differentiated mindset to a growth oriented and humane one.

The curtain that had earlier become the reason for division now becomes the reason for unification. He has also shifted the position of the projection curtain which was earlier placed as a fence between the two sides. Now, the place of the curtain is at the back of the potter's section. This also gives the deprived a chance to witness the movie right in front of them with no hindrances and perfectly placed curtains. The curtain becomes the perfect metaphor for change and growth through this song.

Yeh tara woh tara har tara
Yeh tara woh tara har tara
Dekho jise bhi lage pyara
Yeh tara woh tara har tara
Yeh sab saath mein
Joh hai raat mein
Toh jagmagaya aasman sara
Jagmag taare
Do tare, nau tare, sau tare
Jagmag sare
Har tara hai sharara
Yeh tara woh tara har tara
Yeh tara woh tara har tara
Yeh tara woh tara har tara
Dekho jise bhi lage pyara

The concluding stanza of the song reinstils the message that Mohan has started with. This time, it is the children who are singing and dancing. The chorus starts with the small girl child singing the part of the song. This is also the inclusion of the minority. The girl child is from the section that belongs to the lower caste. Previously, it was Chiku who sang, and danced and he belonged to the upper class. The girl also becomes the symbolic inclusion to give equal rights to girls and not deprive them of the education that they deserve- this is something that he also tells the Panch when he goes to his house and the Panch says that girls are going to be married and only do household chores to which Mohan replies that they are also equally capable of doing anything that a boy can do. This is now executed in the song. The girl sings the song, and she sings it well. This also balances the caste balance and the gender balance. He is giving a chance to everyone which they deserve and opening the times that they lived in before. The girls dance and we see that all the children are dancing with them, forgetting their differences and factors of separation.

Additionally, there is a perfect Jugalbandi that happens between Mohan and the children singing. Mohan sings *Yeh tara woh tara har tara* while the children sing *Dekho jise bhi lage Pyara* and vice versa. This is a perfect way to end as it showcases how they are singing the same song but with differences. It also shows a path wherein sometimes a part is ahead and progressing whereas the other times, they are behind, and others have overtaken them. This is done through children, and they have a massive impact on the audience. This exchange also becomes the legacy that Mohan wishes to leave behind. He might leave the village and ultimately this world but his idea of equality and equal rights would be sung by the children.

Thus, the song becomes an explanation of unity and a reality check wherein the villagers have been differentiating amongst themselves based on caste and occupation. Mohan also signifies the name of Mahatma Gandhi who fought for the rights of the lower caste people. It is also the name of Lord Krishna who would engross the audience to his flute tunes and dance with everyone in the village. Mohan not only instills a message for unity but also encourages them to believe and see things scientifically. He talks about the cosmos and the stars, people and their occupation, and rivers and rainbows. His examples also state a sense of acute observation and learning though nature- something with which villages are closely related to. His ideas are real and something that can be seen and proven unlike the ideas of traditional thinking about the idea of caste discrimination and differences. It is indeed the work of geniuses to come together and convey such a powerful message in around 7 minutes to the world.

19. Yun Hi Chala Chal Rahi- Swades

<u>Independent</u>

Yun Hi Chala Chal Rahi is essentially a fusion. A fusion of the western elements blended seamlessly with the Indian ones. Be it in lyrics or in the way the classical aalaps are present in between the lines, the song becomes a masterpiece in its each stroke. This song serves two purposes in the film- expressing the feelings of Mohan and giving an ideal philosophy to live life.

Yun hi chala chal raahi… (Repeat once)
Kitni hasin hai yeh duniya
Bhool saare jhumele,
Dekh phoolon ke mele
Badi rangeen hai yeh duniya
Rum dum dara rutaaru rum dara…(Repeat 2 times)
Bhaiya

Translation- Oh traveler, come along this way and go ahead on your journey. The world is a beautiful place. Forget your troubles and admire the beauty of the flowers. The world is a colorful place.

The radio voice sets up the mood. They are going to talk about life as a journey. It perfectly juxtaposes with the road trip that Mohan is on. The journey is about forgetting his work at NASA and connecting back to his roots. It also symbolizes the contrast that he has always felt subconsciously. His life in the USA is all about modern life that includes urban wonders such as well-built structures, rockets, and the marvels of space. However, India is all about simple things such as the flowers that make a rangoli of colours or the scenic views of trees and rivers.

The next voice is of Fakir (Makrand Deshpande) who sings an aalap. Notice how subtle and powerful this small aalap is. The radio song is essentially an upbeat western song played on modern instruments. The aalap is a part of Indian music. It subtly shows the transition of Mohan. Also notice how Mohan is surprised by the singing of the jogi but then enjoys it thoroughly. The Jogi becomes the embodiment of India that he is fascinated and attracted to. He is taken back when the Fakir starts singing but, in a moment, or two, he starts appreciating and enjoying it. It is like he knew how interesting India is but he never enjoyed it like he is doing now. The aalap is also the seed of love for India to Mohan. He is listening to it for the first time and is enamored by it. Fakir insists Mohan to sing and continue the song. Mohan is surprised by the request but then finds himself automatically contributing and making his own song on the tune. He goes ahead and gives us a piece of his mind in these lines-

(Yeh rasta hai keh raha ab mujhase
Milane ko hai koi kahin ab tujhse)
Aalap
Dil ko hai kyon yeh betabi kis se mulakaat honi hai
Jiska kab se arman tha shayad wohi baat honi hai

Translation- The path is whispering to me that you are going to meet someone special. My heart jumps in excitement pondering who this special person is. Maybe it is someone who I have always longed to meet.

His lines are that of hope and good company. India is a place where he feels everyone is close to him. He is a person who has not lived for years in India but he knows that he would meet people who would become close to him here. It is also the affection and love that he has for his Kaveri Amma.

Just as he sings this, an aalap joins him. Notice how Mohan's voice is like the one that is between the two varied voices- one western voice played on the radio. The other of the Fakir that is Indian and classical. His is a fine mixture of both and somewhere, it is trying to merge with either of the voices. This becomes the theme of the movie. He thinks that he is the voice that merges smoothly with the one on the radio, and is western, advanced, and not very rooted in India.

It is exactly after the aalap that he expresses his intuition to meet someone special. He thinks that he would meet someone special and take them to the USA and live a happy life.

Yun hi chala chal rahi…(Repeat once)
Jeevan gadi hai samay pahiya
Aansoon ki nadiyan bhi hain, kushiyon ki bagiyan

bhi hain
Rasta sab tera take bhaiya

Translation- Life is a wheel of time. There are rivers of grief and gardens of joy. Everyone is supporting and rooting for you.

Fakir starts singing and his tune becomes that of the radio voice but with an Indian touch of philosophy and some life wisdom. It is also noticeable how the Fakir takes up the tune of Mojan and starts singing on the same lines. It is a connection that they have made. Both are in their own worlds and have their own ways but there is an influence of each on the other.

The lines show us a glimpse of the Indian mindset and the wisdom that is present in India. The very Buddhist idea to perceive happiness and grief as something that shall pass and strive to achieve a state of Shunyata or neutrality is what is reflected here. There is the state of expressing and feeling the emotions to the fullest but not to be carried away in that moment to hope or promise something that is not achievable.

Dekhoon jidhar bhi in raahon mein,
Rang pighalte hain nigaahon mein

Thandi hawa hai, thandi chaanv hai,
Door woh jaane kiska gaanv hai
Badal yeh kaisa chaya, dil yeh kahan le aaya
Sapna yeh kya dikhlaya hai mujhko

Translation- Wherever I glance on the path, I see colors melting in my eyes. The cool breeze and the cool shade soothe my heart. I wonder whose village is that which is far away. What is this fog and where has my heart taken me? What are these dreams that I am witnessing?

The paragraph starts with the same stanza of Yun Hi chala chal rahi and goes ahead. It is like they have crossed a level and now, they are closer to their destination. The path is heartwarming for Mohan. The colors express his heart's desires and soothe it. The wind and the shade act like a balm to his wavering soul. He wonders whose village is it so far. He is also in a state of surprise if whatever he witnesses and experiences is even real. He is in a pleasant shock and wonders if this is a dream.

Notice how these lines also show an awe for the land that he is in. He wanted to visit India to meet his mother but the landscape has made his heart jump in joy. It is the village that makes him happy. He is fascinated by it and he wants to visit it and know more about it. In fact, he considers this as a happy dream that he is experiencing and does not want to wake up. It is one of the rare instances wherein the reality is like a dream and one wants to really wake up and pinch themselves to check.

Har sapna sach lage, jo prem agan jale
Jo raah tu chale apane man ki
Har pal ki seep se moti hi tu chhune
Jo tu sada sune apne man ki

Translation- Every dream shall be true and every desire shall be fulfilled if you ignite the spark of love and if you walk the path that your heart desires. You shall pick up pearls from the streams if you always follow your heart.

He thinks this as a dream when the Fakir tells him that the key to making the dream a reality is just listening to his heart. See how subtly the Fakir is saying that he has been ignoring the call of his heart and he should pay more attention to it, which eventually happens in the movie.

Man apne ko kuch aisa halka paaye,
Jaise kandhon pe rakha bojh hat jaaye
Jaise bhola sa bachpan phir se aaye,
Jaise barson mein koi ganga nahaye…(Repeat once)
Dhul sa gaya hai yeh man,
Khul sa gaya har bandhan
Jeevan ab lagta hai paavan mujhko..

Translation- My heart feels light and relieved. It is as if the burden from my shoulder is removed. It is as if the innocence and joy of childhood has returned. My heart feels relieved and pure as if it has bathed in the holy river of Ganga. Every connection feels revived. My life feels pure and holy.

Mohan then expresses how light he feels because of the place. It's as if someone has lifted the burden and washed away all his sins to give him a new life. Ganga becomes the symbol of his longing and desires. He has finally found that. See how Mohan is extremely awed by India. The idea of bathing in Ganga feels so pure and relieving to him. He has not gone to the shore but he already feels the vibes of purity and relief as soon as he witnesses the expanse of India. The diversity and the expanse is what makes him so comfortable and happy. Mohan does not realize but his heart has always been in India and when it finally reaches there physically, he feels the relief and the joy that he had always been longing for.

Jeevan mein preet hai, honthon pe geet hai
Bas yeh hi jeet hai, sun le rahi
Tu jis disha bhi ja, tu pyaar hi luta
Tu deep hi jala, sun le rahi
Yunhi chala, chal raahi (Repeat once)

Translation- If you have love in your life and song in your heart, you have achieved Nirvana. Listen to me o traveler, you shall spread love and joy no matter where you go!

The Fakir then says that you have found what you are looking for. You have solved the mystery of life and cracked the lock of happiness. He also signals that this is the end of your search and if you shall go ahead in the journey, you might not be happy in your life and would miss this feeling of being complete and relieved. The journey of life shall continue but you should know that this is the direction that you have to pursue and go ahead.

Kaun ye mujhko pukaare
Nadiya pahaad jheel aur jharne, jangal aur waadi
In mein hai kiske ishaare
Yeh rasta hai kah raha ab mujhse

Milne ko hai koi kahin ab tujhse
Rum dum daaraa rutaaru rum daaraa…(Repeat 2
times)
Fakir Aalap

SRK Aalap

Yun hi chala chal rahi…(Repeat once)
Kitni hasin hai yeh duniya…

Translation- Who is calling me now? It feels as if the mountains, rivers, and valleys are hinting me to go to someone. The path is telling me that I shall meet someone. I shall go ahead on this path and experience this lovely world!

Mohan is feeling the calling that the land has to him. He feels it very strongly and sees it in each of the beautiful structures, be it the river, mountain, or valley. He is unsure that the calling is from his motherland and he ponders who is calling him.

See how there is a perfect harmony of the three voices now. The western by A R Rahman, the Indian by Kailesh Kher, and the fusion by Udit Narayan. The western voice starts with a voice that mumbles in the western style. Rum Dum Taan becomes that voice.

Then, Fakir starts singing in the classical tune and we hear a beautiful Aalap. But do notice how the Aalap is immediately picked up and continued by Mohan. It is like an immediate impulsive creation that he does not realize. This also surprises Fakir. This repeats again and both are in harmony with each other. They do not know but they have imbibed each other's influence and are becoming a different person. In fact, Mohan does not even realize that he is now in love with the Aalap and not with the western beats. Just like he does not realize his love for the village and his homeland in the movie.

As the song ends, there is a tune on the trumpet. The tune fades out the song and gives it a final high but then, we hear a very Indian instrument like Ektara which concludes the song. See how the instrument foreshadows what the end is. It is the Indian tune that has won over the heart of Mohan and he would soon be singing the same.

Then the Jogi leaves, leaving behind a changed Mohan who is yet to feel the change.

That was the magic of geniuses like Rahman, Gowariker, Udit Narayan, and Kailesh Kher. The lyrical magic is done by the Maestro- Javed Akhtar. Swades was a treat to watch and such a deeply positive, impactful, and touching film. Waiting for more films like this!

20. Kinare- Queen

<u>Recommended</u>

Queen-
Coming of age is a term that is used to describe a person's journey from being a child to adult. This is a very loose and generic meaning. However, if we try to look at it in a deeper way, the term means a person's transition from being a dependent, hesitant, nervous, and diffident person to becoming an independent, confident, free spoken, and courageous one.

Did the above become too theoretical? Do not worry if you did not get it. Just see the film Queen and you will know exactly what coming of age means. Queen is a film that traces the journey of Kangana Ranaut from being a small-town girl who is diffident and limited to her own surroundings to her becoming an independent girl who goes to Paris all by herself because her wedding was called off by the groom. The song that is analyzed is a part of the film and it is absolute proof of who Kangana (Rani) has become as her trip in Paris is coming to an end.

There are no spoilers. However, watching the movie is highly recommended as the movie is one of the best in Bollywood. The song is brilliant in all aspects and what pulled my attention to it was the perfect composition, super inspiring lyrics, and the brilliant cinematography that the song has.

Dhoonde har ek saans mein
Dubkiyon ke baagh mein
Har bhanwar ke paas kinare

Translation- In every breath and dip, I try to find the shore of calmness and support. I look around fanatically for it.

This stanza describes her mental outlook when she first started the journey. Kinare here can refer to Support and someone to rely on. The original meaning is a shore, which also goes perfectly with the meaning. The visual in the video shows Kangana walking alone and trying to embrace the feeling that she has. She is finding what she feels (dhunde har ek saans mein).

Beh rahe jo saath mein
Jo hamare khaas the
Kar gaye, apni baat kinare

Translation- The people I knew and loved, the people I trusted and leaned on, left me in the middle of a chaos to suffer.

The person she loved and who would be the special someone in her life- Rajkumar Rao, left her in the middle and went on his own way to the shore. It also means that because of that, she had to go on the honeymoon alone. However, she is now realizing how good the turn of events was for her. She smiles on figuring out the newfound self and instead of cribbing on the incident, she has a huge ear to ear grin as to how being alone meant loving oneself and being proud of what you are.

Gar maanjhi saath mein
Ger ho bhi jaaye
Toh khud hi toh pathwaar ban
Paar hoge hum

Translation- Even if everyone else leaves me in the boat sail of life, I shall be the sailor who sails the ocean by myself.

This is her decision to go on and take up the journey all alone even if the marriage has been called off. She has decided that she would be her own support and complete the journey. (*Toh khud hi toh pathwaar ban Paar hoge hum).* See how symbolic and powerful the visual is. Just look at how the cinematographer translates *"paar hona"* which is overcoming something and coming out successfully to Kangana running out of the gate with a huge smile on her face. Even though everyone left her, she has come out of the situation successfully and more importantly, happily.

Jo choti si har ek nahar
Sagar ban bhi jaaye
Koi tinka leke haath mein
Dhoond hi lenge hum

Translation- Even if each of the smallest waves transform into giant storms, I shall lean on the smallest ray of hope to finally find my shore

The symbolism is quite evident here where the cinematographer quite literally presents the water body for the embodiment of "Sagar", an ocean in the scene. She is running alone and there is only a bit for support. She has started to realize how the journey has changed her, and she is enjoying her newfound self to the fullest.

Kinare…
Kinare…

Kinare…

Even though this is just a word in a repeated manner, the cinematographer finds a beautiful way to symbolize her journey. See the variety of places she runs through. There is a narrow street that would immediately remind you of the looting incident that happened with her in the movie. She is running happily and successfully through it. That was probably an incident where any human would have given up, but she fought until the end and came out victorious. This also symbolizes how she did *everything alone, including getting rid of that goon.*

Khud hi toh hai hum
Kinare…
Kaise honge kam
Kinare…
Hain jahaan hai hum
Kinare…
Khud hi toh hai hum
Haan… khud hi toh hai hum

Translation- We ourselves are the shore. How shall they reduce or disappear when we are there, standing firm? We are the shore, and nothing can change that

This stanza juxtaposes with her crossing the street. See how confidently and easily she is doing so. Remember the point in the movie where she could not move ahead in Paris because of the traffic. This is a superb yet very subtle way of showing her growth and how a drastic change has made her the "Rani" or the queen. Also, notice how the lyrics are becoming more and more self-assuring. The peak of the buildup are the lines – *"Khud hi toh hai hum Haan… khud hi toh hai hum"*. She herself is the journey and the destination. For a few seconds, she runs to the club where her friends are.
This is the place where I have goosebumps whenever I have the song. This is the sitar tune that launches a Tsunami like wave of happiness, strong enough to drown you in tears of happiness. Absolutely no words and no strong actions, this is a place that sums it all. She has reached the club (the metaphorical end of the journey), she is happy, and she is finding her friends. Do note the blend of emotions she is going through. Her confidence is keeping her happy but there is a slight anxiety of not being able to spot her friends immediately.
Hear the soft and pleasing sitar fading away to make

way for the pleasant and dearing saxophone that is perfectly blended with the goodbye hugs to her friends. This is a mixed moment. There is a sadness of separation but there is the joy of friendship and strong bonds. They have found a world separate from where they lived, and they know that they are there for each other irrespective of how far they are!

Kinare…
Kinare…
Kinare…
Khud hi toh hai hum
Kinaare…
Kaise honge kam
Kinare…
Hain jahaan hai hum
Kinare…
Khud hi toh hai hum
Haan…khud hi toh hai hum

Then comes the final stanza of the song. This scene of like 5 seconds sums up the drastic change in her life. Her friends have left, and you can see the sadness, nervousness, and a feeling of being lost alone. However, she looks above to God, says thank you for the journey and then jumps up with joy. She has moved on. The journey has made her what she always wanted to be but could not. She has become Rani. She has become **Queen**.

Hats off to people like Amit Trivedi (music composer), Kangana Ranaut(actor), Mohan Kanan(singer), Vikas Bahl (director), and Bobby Singh (Cinematographer) for creating a masterpiece like this.

Khud hi toh hai hum… Kinare

Epilogue

This brings us to the end of the book. Do remember that this is a series of song analyses that I would keep on writing as and when time permits. This is part one and essentially the first attempt to bring the song analyses that I usually put up on my blog to a print form.

I would sincerely thank you for supporting my venture and you having taken the efforts to read the book and go ahead and dive deeper into the world of cinema with my lenses. I would love to hear your views and ideas about the same. Also, any and every song suggestion that you would give helps me to bring new content to you as well as exercise my own brain to go into the unfound depths of the movies and the songs. The beauty lies when I see the song and the movie a couple of times and realize so many things that I would have missed in the first time.

I hope India produces more and more cinematic masterpieces that would lead us to think better and eventually, help us to be better human beings!